MEANING
MAKING

8 Values That Drive America's Newest Generations

Josh Packard, PhD
Ellen B. Koneck, MAR
Jerry Ruff, MA
Megan Bissell, MA
Jana N. Abdulkadir

Foreword by Rabbi Elan Babchuck, MBA

Springtide
RESEARCH INSTITUTE

Created by the publishing team of Springtide Research Institute.

Copyright © 2020 by Springtide Research Institute, 2626 E 82nd Street, Suite 203, Bloomington, MN, springtideresearch.org. All rights reserved. No part of this book may be reproduced by any means without the written permission of the publisher.

Printed in the United States of America

5929

ISBN 978-1-64121-090-4

Library of Congress Cataloging-in-Publication Data
Names: Packard, Josh, author. | Koneck, Ellen B., author. | Ruff, Jerry, author. | Bissell, Megan, author. | Abdulkadir, Jana N., author.
Title: Meaning making : 8 values that drive America's newest generations / Josh Packard, PhD, Ellen B. Koneck, MAR, Jerry Ruff, MA, Megan Bissell, MA, Jana N. Abdulkadir ; Foreword by Rabbi Elan Babchuck, MBA.
Description: Bloomington : Springtide Research Institute, [2020] |
Identifiers: LCCN 2020025591 (print) | LCCN 2020025592 (ebook) | ISBN 9781641210904 (paperback) | ISBN 9781641211369 (ebook) | ISBN 9781641211376 (epub)
Subjects: LCSH: Values—United States—History—21st century. | Ethics—United States—History—21st century. | Youth—United States—Attitudes—History—21st century. | Generation Z—History—21st century.
Classification: LCC BJ352 .P34 2020 (print) | LCC BJ352 (ebook) | DDC 303.3/7208350973—dc23
LC record available at https://lccn.loc.gov/2020025591
LC ebook record available at https://lccn.loc.gov/2020025592

ACKNOWLEDGMENTS

I owe many thanks to many people for the existence of this book.

First, and most importantly, I thank the young people who responded to our surveys, the young people who told us their stories in interviews, and the young people in our own lives—to whom this book is ultimately dedicated. The hope and motivation behind all the work we do at Springtide is to serve you. We undertake this service both by amplifying your voices, stories, and values, and by equipping the people and organizations in your life to serve you better.

Next, a note of gratitude for the organizations and examples highlighted throughout these pages. In a rapidly changing world, we set out to find and hold up new spaces that are emerging to meet the needs and encourage the values we hear young people expressing. These organizations—and the people who lead them—are on the cutting edge of care. We admire your work and hope to translate the spirit of your innovation so that others might follow your lead.

Finally, to the researchers, writers, editors, and designers who are responsible for each sentence, idea, data point, and detail: Ellen B. Koneck, head writer and editor; Jerry Ruff, former managing editor; Megan Bissell, head researcher; Jana N. Abdulkadir, social science research intern; and so many more. Books are always a team effort, and this was certainly true for this book. I especially want to thank Rabbi Elan Babchuck, a member of the Springtide Research Advisory Board and a role model in creative and expansive thinking in service of young people and others. We are grateful for your help, both providing feedback in the building of this book and for your eloquent and humbling words of introduction.

—Josh Packard, Executive Director

CONTENTS

FOREWORD

In my role at Glean Network, a think tank focused on developing and equipping innovators and entrepreneurs to imagine and develop the future of faith in America, I spend a lot of time looking at numbers. The think tank studies statistics, deciphers data, and ultimately tries to craft narratives that inspire hope and spark thoughtful action on the part of spiritual, business, and social impact leaders around the country. The American religious landscape is shifting so rapidly—the rate of disruption is only accelerating—and making sense of those shifts is the first step toward better serving the people behind those numbers.

One of the challenges of parsing these numbers, however, is that we must rely on the accepted labels and categories used by the researchers. For years I've listened to colleagues and friends refer to almost a third of the population in America as "nones." Others focus on the "unaffiliated," the "nonbelievers," the "nonreligious."

While these typologies might offer convenient and clean ways of understanding the world, they end up defining people by who and what they are *not*. What these labels gloss over is the humanity of each individual seeking to make meaning of an increasingly indecipherable world, to discover their purpose in life, and to feel known during a time of growing anonymity.

This book reminds us that we can do better. *Meaning Making* introduces us to people—*real people*—whose lived experiences and deepest yearnings paint vivid pictures that numbers and labels alone could never do. This approach allows humanity to tell the story about numbers—and not the other way around.

Meaning Making is an invitation for innovators in every sector—from tech to education to religion—to design around the deeply felt needs of our nation's youth. It invites entrepreneurs—from venture-backed to social to spiritual—to build on the solid foundation provided in these chapters.

Meaning Making doesn't just outline these emerging opportunities to meet the needs of young people; it hands us a blueprint to build a world worthy of them. And while much of the work of innovation and entrepreneurship might rely on counting people, this book reminds us to make sure that those people count.

Rabbi Elan Babchuck, MBA
Founding Director, Glean Network
Director of Innovation, Clal

INTRODUCTION

Young people care deeply about _____.

For many of us, how we fill in that blank, consciously or subconsciously, will determine our work and relationships with young people. If we get it wrong, our service to and with young people will suffer. At Springtide Research Institute, we are determined to get it right, and we undertook research and conversations with young people to do just that.

Meaning Making: 8 Values That Drive America's Newest Generations is our investigation into the values that young people, ages 13 to 25, practice and uphold. What motivates them in their common quest to discover, create, and express significant meaning in their lives? What organizations and groups do they choose to engage with and be a part of? How do those organizations exhibit and express those values?

The values young people articulated comprise the chapters of this book. They emerged from surveys and interviews with young people, as well as other quantitative and qualitative research involving a range of resources, both scholarly and popular. As we collected our data early in 2020 through a nationally representative survey; looked at other data sources; and uncovered the practices, people, and organizations that were attracting intense commitment from young people; we made discoveries helpful to leaders trying to shape organizations, groups, institutions, and one-on-one relationships that better serve and care for young people today.

In many ways, the young people represented in the research in this book[1] are simply continuing social trends that have been ongoing for years. Our society has moved away from lives neatly

---

[1] At Springtide, we are committed to understanding the full breadth and depth of experiences of young people. The research in this book includes surveys and interviews with young people from ages 13 to 25. Internal analysis of survey results revealed no significant differences in terms of values based on age.

organized by traditional institutions. Instead, people have been turning toward new types of organizations and toward personal relationships that permit and encourage living out their entire value system in a variety of ways.

In other words, productive, meaningful work is no longer just the domain of the 9-to-5 job.

Religious belief and spiritual aspirations, explorations, and expressions no longer belong only to Sunday mornings or Friday evenings.

Being a good citizen is not confined to volunteer work done after hours.

The research, stories, advice, and solutions articulated in these chapters confirm that young people are thinking about their lives in holistic ways, where traditional institutional boundaries have been blurred or erased entirely.

These social trends have significant implications for leaders who work with young people, including employers, religious leaders, teachers, youth program workers, and social entrepreneurs. Whatever your role, you can't go wrong by attending to and adopting the eight values articulated by young people in this book.

Accountable. Inclusive. Authentic. Welcoming. Impactful. Relational. Growthful. Meaningful.

Each of these values consistently emerged for young people both in terms of their personal practices and what they hope to see embodied and embraced in organizations, causes, or clubs they join. The converse is true as well. Absent these values, organizations, groups, and relationships run the real risk of alienating young people or not attracting them in the first place. But these values aren't just for or about young people. Rather, taking a cue from their principles, the work of creating a culture that is accountable, inclusive, authentic, welcoming, impactful,

relational, growthful, and meaningful will benefit and improve your organization and relationships in countless ways.

Throughout this book, we identify and explain these values, and we pull from a variety of sources to illustrate exactly how these values show up and matter in practice. You will find personal narratives, data, definitions, and case studies in each chapter. Additionally, at Springtide Research Institute, we aim to provide *actionable* insights. To that end, you'll also find prompts to help you incorporate and reflect on the ways to embed or strengthen these values in your own work and relationships with young people, as well as references for learning more about them.

Young people are seeking meaning, and they are looking in new places and looking to new people to find and create it. Through an exploration of these eight values they hold in high regard, we hope to equip you to meet and aid young people in that quest, and to add meaning to your organization, relationships, and life in the process.

CHAPTER 1

ACCOUNTABLE

Away at college, Ellie experienced an unnerving and confusing sense of displacement and disconnection in her life. Friends, family, and familiar activities and commitments—those bedrock connections that had grounded her and provided a sense of accountability to both herself and the trusted people and associations in her life—were now distant.

"I knew who I was and what I loved to do in high school, but then I got to college and other people's interests were different, their thoughts were different," Ellie says. Without the daily presence of these trusted adults, friends, and routines, and without a clear sense of purpose, role, and expectations to hold her accountable, she felt uncertain and unmoored.

Ellie tried various on-campus activities, but found these student-led communities lacked a level of accountability she found essential when choosing where to spend her time. "There was not always a consistent welcoming authority," she explained; a kind of warm presence and familiar face that notices, names, and knows those who show up for the activity. Students don't "always show up or follow through with responsibilities. Communities I thought I would enjoy—such as floor nights, student clubs, dances, floor dinners—did not maintain a level of commitment or consistency from the participants."

Ellie tried adult-led organizations and activities as well. As a musician, she became involved with conservatory and the band ensemble. As a person of faith, she tried worship communities and Scripture study group. As an athlete, she found a gym and workout buddies.

But missing still was the sense that these were people and organizations to whom she might entrust herself—people she could trust to hold her accountable—to encourage her to show up and to check in with her when she didn't. It wasn't until a caring, demanding, trustworthy coach stepped in that Ellie would find the confidence and motivation to thrive at college. Notably, it wasn't this individual's charisma that made the difference, but rather the value of accountability this leader and his organization represented, a value that a majority of young people have told us they seek out in the organizations and activities in which they participate.

We will return to Ellie's story later in the chapter, but first, let's take a look at what accountability means and why it's important to so many young people when choosing the types of organizations and groups to join.

ACCOUNTABILITY
Insights from Springtide Research

The stereotype that young people just want permission, even affirmation, to do "what they want when they want" has persisted for a long time, perhaps especially in American culture. And like many stereotypes, it contains a hint of truth—as young people move from childhood to adulthood, more and more freedoms become available to them. Responsibility amid those freedoms often follows closely behind, though there can be a lag—hence the stereotype.

But, as in Ellie's story, young people have another persistent desire that doesn't get nearly the same spotlight, despite data suggesting its prevalence. Accountability, the all-important value Ellie was seeking in various groups and relationships when she arrived at college, is understood by social scientists as having three parts. A person or organization practicing the value of accountability provides each of these:

1. Clear roles and expectations

2. Well-defined goals and purpose

3. Opportunities for regular and meaningful feedback

Accountability emerges in Springtide survey data as one of the chief values young people seek out when forming relationships with people and places, whether that value is exemplified formally or informally. Often, accountability is rooted in the very culture of an organization, and the character of leadership plays a critical role. In particular, our data suggest that young people value many aspects of accountability—working toward defined goals, owning one's mistakes, making amends, following group norms, and being trustworthy.

Nearly 75%
of respondents said **accountability** is an important quality for any organization they might join.

SPRINGTIDE™ NATIONAL RESEARCH RESULTS
© 2020 Springtide. Cite, share, and join the conversation at springtideresearch.org.

When asked about accountability, young people overwhelmingly indicated that it is highly important to them that the people and organizations in their lives help to hold them and others responsible to the commitments they've made. In fact, nearly 75% of our survey respondents say accountability is a top value in their lives. This high regard for accountability was somewhat surprising to us, as it's not typically a value many people associate with younger generations. But the numbers tell a different story.

Our research also reveals a strong connection between accountability and organizational trust: 45% of young people say that if the leader is not accountable, then they cannot trust the organization; 65% say important qualities of a strong, accountable leader are owning mistakes and making things right.

Furthermore, the value young people place on being accountable extends to their personal lives: 66% of those surveyed believe in taking responsibility for their mistakes and making things right when they've harmed someone.

How can this necessary sense of accountability be conveyed or built? Leaders can begin by establishing clear roles and expectations, providing well-defined goals and purpose, and incorporating opportunities for regular and meaningful feedback. In the next three sections, we look at each of these three aspects of accountability in contexts specific to young people.

CLEAR ROLES AND EXPECTATIONS

Organizational and group settings benefit from clearly defined roles and expectations for participants and leaders alike. Some settings are more emotionally charged than others, heightening the need for this sort of clarity. The Dinner Party—a movement that gathers young people who have lost loved ones—is a case in point.

Hard losses can be difficult to discuss, even among the best of friends or with the most trusted adults. Often in larger groups, this is even more challenging, as sharing vulnerably about a deep, perhaps even still raw, wound is risky. **That's why ground rules—the first facet of accountability—are so important.**

When people gather with the express goal of talking about deep grief and loss, it is helpful, maybe even necessary, to have clear guidance, some rules of conversation for sharing such confidences. This Dinner Party provides a fine example.

Lennon Flowers lost her mom to lung cancer during her senior year of college. Three years later, Lennon had moved 3,000 miles from home—but not away from the need to continue to talk about her mom and explore how her life, death, and absence continued to affect Lennon. Then Carla Fernandez, a friend who had also lost a parent at a young age, invited her over for dinner. From that seed was born The Dinner Party, a now worldwide community of 20- and 30-somethings who have each experienced the loss of someone deeply significant in their lives. The hosted dinners give participants an empathetic, listening, and compassionate space in which "to transform life after loss from an isolating experience into one marked by community support, candid conversation, and forward movement using the age-old practice of breaking bread," according to The Dinner Party.

Today, with more than 3,000 currently active participants at more than 275 tables in over 100 cities and towns worldwide, The Dinner Party has developed simple but significant expectations to guide Dinner Partiers, which are posted on its website:

- **Stick with "I" statements and avoid advice-giving.** Remember that no two stories are ever the same.

- **Share the air.** We listen to silence as well as speech, and you are under no obligation to speak: In the words of our friends at The Center for Courage & Renewal, this is not a "share or die" group.

- **Keep it confidential.** What's said at the table stays at the table.

- **No grief wars.** Parent loss or partner loss. Sudden loss or years of caregiving. No one's grief is "better" or "worse" than another's. We're here to hold space for all of our stories, not just our own.

- **Joy and sadness are not mutually exclusive.** We welcome laughter here as much as we welcome tears.

For young people in their 20s and 30s, significant grief is uncommon. Those attending a Dinner Party might already feel like outsiders among their peers. This is why, when navigating the murky and messy experience of grief, practicing accountability is of the utmost importance for participants to feel safe and encouraged. Indeed, in *any* group or organization where difficult or self-revealing conversations are valued and encouraged—a faith-sharing group at a church, a candid performance review conversation at work—shared accountability to the inviolable dignity of fellow participants is an absolute must.

The framework developed by The Dinner Party is impressive for many reasons. For example, it establishes the heart and values of the gathering. It also expresses some ground rules of effective communication and establishes norms around discussing a topic where clear social norms don't always exist or conversation is particularly challenging.

> **"** In *any* group or organization where difficult and often self-revealing conversations are valued and encouraged, shared accountability to the inviolable dignity of fellow participants is an absolute must. **"**

Such a clear framework in this discussion on accountability provides a model for how we might operate in our own lives and as leaders of groups or organizations where young people are involved. The Dinner Party establishes clear roles and expectations for all parties. The Dinner Party works because participants know exactly what they can expect from one another and themselves, and they have this mutually accepted guide to refocus the gathering, gently correct themselves or others in the group, and even discern how to approach the night together in the first place.

> **ACT ⟩ ON THE DATA:** A public display of roles and expectations, such as on a website, whiteboard, and so on, can serve as a reminder and hold leaders as well as members mutually accountable to one another and to the goal or purpose for which the organization exists.

SHARED GOAL OR PURPOSE

The value of accountability deals with expectations, responsibilities, and communication. A shared goal or purpose is essential for practicing this value, whether within an organization or a relationship. For a group or organization to thrive, goals for leaders and members alike must align at some level.

What happens when one side of that equation—leadership or membership—moves away from an original goal or purpose for participation? Quite understandably, accountability may suffer, and with it the reason for participation. Without clarity or agreement about *why* to gather, the inclination to keep doing so understandably decreases.

Leaders who work with young people over an extended period often witness participation falling off as the young people grow up. These leaders might ask themselves what's behind the decline: Are participants "aging out" of an organization or activity for unavoidable and even good reasons that accompany human development? Or has a discrepancy, even a clash, about the expectations and goals of the activity occurred among members and leaders? Participation in youth sports illustrates the challenge for leaders who work with young people. Studies in recent years have documented a steady drop-off in involvement in both school and nonschool programs from the late preteens through high school.

What seems to be contributing to this decline, studies conducted by the Aspen Institute, George Washington University ("The Fun Integration Theory"), and others suggest, is that the *original shared goal* or purpose of having fun, maintaining a reasonable balance of sports with other life activities, and ensuring ease of access regardless of individual ability (inclusion), had morphed. Increasingly, young people were being turned off by the pressure on winning, the demanding practice schedules that left little time for other interests, and the favoritism shown toward the most gifted athletes.

While you may not be involved with youth sports, clear lessons are here for leaders of all kinds of organizations. One of the more notorious examples of a decline of young people from organizational participation is in religion. Leaders who work with young people in this arena might ask themselves whether there is simply an overall difference between the goals and purpose of most organized religion and those of the young people they might wish to serve. If the answer is yes, how might this be addressed? Further, if the decline in participation follows along a continuum of age, as statistics seem to suggest, when and how and why does this trend manifest itself over time?

Any group or organization that seeks to serve young people ought to regularly investigate whether the goals and purposes of members and the organization align. Be clear to yourself, as well as the young people you care for, regarding your agendas. As for understanding the agendas of the young people themselves: ask them. This brings us to the third aspect that defines the value of accountability.

ACT **ON THE DATA:** Regularly review the goals and purposes of your group or organization, with leadership and membership as well. Be both humble and flexible, willing to change when change is called for, to adjust methods and procedures as circumstances merit, and even to dissolve if a goal has been accomplished or an original purpose no longer exists.

REGULAR, MEANINGFUL FEEDBACK

Young people need to have opportunities for regular and honest feedback to feel that they are being afforded the two-way accountability they desire and deserve. Almost two-thirds of young people surveyed by Springtide expect leaders of organizations to make amends for wrongdoings and to take ownership of mistakes. Nearly the same percentage of young people (66%) indicate that they apply those same high standards of accountability to themselves personally. Clearly, accountability is understood as a value to be shouldered and practiced *together*.

65% say important qualities of a strong, **accountable leader are owning mistakes and making things right** within an organization.

45% say that if **the leader is not accountable,** they **cannot trust the organization.**

SPRINGTIDE™ NATIONAL RESEARCH RESULTS
© 2020 Springtide. Cite, share, and join the conversation at springtideresearch.org.

In Australia, an effort is underway to open a two-way street for communication around accountability, ensuring young people have the opportunity to speak and to be heard. Creating and sustaining a culture of accountability is one of the goals of

Helen Connolly, the first-ever Commissioner for Children and Young People in South Australia. Convinced that accountability requires effective feedback mechanisms and that young people are critical stakeholders of governments, businesses, and communities, Connolly set out to talk to young people ages 13 to 18 about their views and experiences. She writes about the experience in a 2018 article in the online journal *Medium*.

Trust was a recurring theme in these conversations, Connolly reports. She heard from young people that they are more likely to trust governments, businesses, and schools if those institutions ask for and respond to feedback. One 16-year-old girl she talked with explained that "feedback must be there for everyone. . . . Responses to feedback must be fast, efficient, reliable and must cater to the needs of whoever needs assistance." The mechanism for feedback can't be in vain—young people can see right through empty gestures. Instead, as the young woman indicates, there must be opportunities for *meaningful* feedback, which means it is taken seriously and responded to thoughtfully.

66 The mechanism for feedback can't be in vain—
young people can see right through empty
gestures. Instead . . . there must be opportunities
for *meaningful* feedback, which means it is taken
seriously and responded to thoughtfully. **99**

Young people expect leaders and organizations to hold themselves and others accountable for working toward defined goals. Young people are willing to hold themselves to this high standard—to take responsibility for mistakes and make amends if they've done wrong. It's no surprise they also expect this from leaders and organizations—indeed, 45% of our survey respondents report that if a leader *doesn't practice* the value of accountability, the organization cannot be trusted.

If young people are allowed meaningful and regular feedback, they can do their part to ensure accountability in leadership, in organizations, and in their fellow members. Given this opportunity for feedback, young people are far less likely to feel patronized. And there is no surer way to alienate young people than to patronize them.

ACT ▶ ON THE DATA: Feedback that goes nowhere can be more deflating than helpful. Ensure that feedback is actionable and, if needed, assist members in strategizing and implementing an informed response.

GETTING BACK ON TRACK

Midway through college, Ellie felt she was doing poorly, both physically and emotionally. Not unlike many young people who leave home for the first time to attend a higher education institution, Ellie was at a distance from the people and activities that had played important roles in keeping her accountable before. She found herself needing feedback in the midst of developing new routines, discerning her commitments, and discovering an evolving purpose.

Ellie knew what she was seeking: relationships that practiced accountability. She looked to several caring adults to help ground and support her. Among them were her mother, a close faculty friend, a Scripture study host, and her gym coach. Through their deep listening, helpful direction, and trustworthy warmth and support, they helped restore Ellie to renewed health and well-being.

One of the critical supports in Ellie's life was a coach in the highly accountable culture of her small gym. This coach, along with her workout buddies, embodied the critical elements that comprise the three aspects of accountability.

Working Out a Culture of Accountability

With the emergence of boutique, online, and garage gyms, amid other innovations, the health club industry has changed dramatically in recent decades. Many of the most successful gyms have in common a culture of accountability. This makes sense for workout communities: it takes hard work to keep showing up to get healthy and strong, and a culture of accountability can aid that work.

Greg Amundson, a well-known coach, explains in an article in *The CrossFit Journal* the way accountability serves his community: "When an athlete communicates goals to a coach and fellow athletes, a relationship is formed based upon trust and accountability. The athlete becomes accountable to . . . give 100 percent on the path to accomplishing the goal . . . [and] puts a high amount of trust in the coach and community to keep him or her accountable to the stated goal." As Amundson says, making goals public builds not only accountability but trust, both critical elements in building strong relationships with and among young people.

Ellie says her gym became "a family or at least a group of people who pushed me to be better and were very caring and worried about my state of being." Their concern took the form of accountability: "I felt comfortable to walk into this place and share my concerns because we were comrades who had consistently shown up to our class and worked together. We have conquered hard workouts together, relieved stress, and become more comfortable with talking through deeper things with one another."

During a difficult season, Ellie wasn't keeping the commitments she'd made. "I was not going to the gym as much," she admitted. Observing this, her coach approached her and invited her to train with him at 7:00 a.m., before her first class. "Then go home and eat your breakfast," he told her, "just come in and do it." As Ellie remarked, "It was just that daily motivation" of the coach pushing her to keep coming in and to take care of herself that helped turn her around.

Ellie's mother, a beloved faculty mentor, her Scripture study host, a coach: together, this constellation of adults helped to hold Ellie accountable to the person she wanted to be. "They were a family, or at least a group of people who pushed me to be better and were very caring and worried about my state of being," says Ellie. "They all encouraged me to be better, to keep moving forward." They held Ellie accountable.

> **"** They all encouraged me to be better,
> to keep moving forward. **"**
> —Ellie

BRINGING IT ALL TOGETHER

Takeaways

1. Young people overwhelmingly indicate—indeed, nearly 75% of respondents—that it is important to them that the people and organizations in their lives help to hold them and others responsible to the commitments they've made. Fully 66% of young people hold themselves to standards of high accountability, too.

2. Hard losses can be difficult to discuss, even among the best of friends or with the most trusted adults. Often in larger groups, this is even more challenging, as sharing vulnerably about a deep, perhaps even still raw, wound is risky. That's why ground rules—the first facet of accountability—are so important.

3. In *any* group or organization where difficult or self-revealing conversations are valued and encouraged—a faith-sharing group at a church, a candid performance review conversation at work—shared accountability to the inviolable dignity of fellow participants is an absolute must.

4. The value of accountability deals with expectations, responsibilities, and communication. Among many other places, we looked at the importance of accountability in The Dinner Party's guidelines, the varied expectations impacting youth sports, and the two-way opportunity for feedback for young people in Australia.

5. The mechanism for feedback can't be in vain—young people can see right through empty gestures. Instead . . . there must be opportunities for meaningful feedback, which is taken seriously and responded to thoughtfully.

✓ Act on the Data

❑ A public display of roles and expectations, such as on a website, whiteboard, and so on, can serve as a reminder and hold leaders as well as members mutually accountable to one another and to the goal or purpose for which the organization exists.

❑ Regularly review the goals and purposes of your group or organization, with leadership and membership as well. Be both humble and flexible, willing to change when change is called for, to adjust methods and procedures as circumstances merit, and even to dissolve if a goal has been accomplished or an original purpose no longer exists.

❑ Feedback that goes nowhere can be more deflating than helpful. Ensure that feedback is actionable and, if needed, assist members in strategizing and implementing an informed response.

Reflect on Your Experience

- Recall a recent experience related to accountability in your organization. Were the three elements of accountability present? If yes, how? If no, what was missing?

- To what extent does interpersonal accountability contribute to a culture of accountability in youth-serving organizations you are familiar with?

- Are you aware of activities or programs in your community that young people tend to drift away from over time, despite intentions to continue to serve them? Try to identify the dynamics of accountability in these organizations. Does this analysis illumine reasons? Does it provide insight into the needs of these young people?

REFERENCES

Amundson, Greg. "Coaching the Mental Side of CrossFit," *The CrossFit Journal*, July 2010.

Connolly, Helen. "Children and Young People Deserve Our Accountability," *Medium*, September 28, 2018.

The Dinner Party. The information about The Dinner Party in this chapter is taken from the "About Us" and "FAQ" sections on the organization's website.

Sport for All, Play for Life: A Playbook to Get Every Kid in the Game. The Aspen Institute Project Play, 2015.

"Survey: Kids Quit Most Sports by Age 11." Aspen Institute Project Play, August 1, 2019.

Visek, Amanda J., et al. "The Fun Integration Theory: Towards Sustaining Children and Adolescents Sport Participation," *Journal of Physical Activity & Health*, 2014.

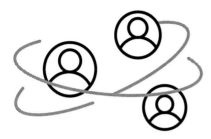

CHAPTER 2

INCLUSIVE

When Peter was accepted into an Ivy League university, he admitted he had "an idealistic vision of what an Ivy League would be like." Though he anticipated his lower socio-economic background would come with some challenges, he also "assumed that the school had worked to diversify their student body, because having an elite institution full of wealthy people isn't the best look." Colleges are natural hubs for meaningful ideas, exchanges, and encounters with people of all backgrounds. Top-tier institutions, it seems fair to assume, could take up that cause with greater resources and energy than most.

Peter arrived at school with a goal "to make the world a better place in any way possible." He hoped he'd have this fundamental principle in common with his classmates: "I thought everybody wanted to do what I did. I went to my university hoping to make the connections necessary to do that."

In a college setting, those connections might be between new ideas in the classroom or among new people in dorms, sports, or clubs. But building new relationships with his peers proved difficult for Peter: "I realized a lot of wealthy kids were there to party or because their families wanted them to continue some legacy," he explained. They were there for utterly different reasons than Peter—not because they wanted to change the world or even get a world-class education. Many seemed to be there simply because they could be. They "were accepted because their parents donated millions of dollars," Peter said.

The disconnect between Peter's own economic background and that of his classmates strained any feeling of welcome, support, or respect he might have experienced upon being accepted to the university. "A lot of students didn't understand why I couldn't take a $40 Uber. They didn't get why I couldn't afford a $300 plane ticket to go home for spring break, while they [took vacations]." This vast difference in wealth made building relationships difficult, Peter remarked. And relationships are one of the most important things a person gains during their undergraduate years.

Peter was accepted to this prestigious university not *because* of but certainly *in light of* the diverse background, perspective, ideas, and worldview he could bring to the institution. But the invitation to attend—the chance to be included—was not inclusive. A commitment to diversity, including socioeconomic diversity, without structures in place to welcome, support, and respect the distinct challenges and benefits that comes with it, is not inclusive—it's tokenism. Peter was left to navigate the culture and class issues on his own, while still shouldering the day-to-day work of undergraduate life.

What would real inclusion have looked and felt like if Peter had arrived to a campus ready to welcome, support, and respect the unique gifts and challenges he brought? How could an organization anticipate the opportunity to create inclusive environments—spaces that bend and flex to meet new and unforeseen needs—so that a commitment to diversity doesn't slide, inadvertently, into the pitfalls of tokenism? The first step in answering these questions is to learn more about what the value of inclusivity means, and where we can see examples of it.

INCLUSIVITY
Insights from Springtide Research

It's not surprising that inclusivity is sometimes mistaken for diversity—and vice versa. They share a common value, which is to bring together and hold space for a variety of people and ideas. But diversity without inclusivity, as in the example of Peter, merely prizes the appearance or gesture of letting lots of people through the door, but it doesn't necessarily welcome, support, or respect those differences in a meaningful way. Imagine a church that prides itself on inviting other-abled individuals to worship but neglects to build a wheelchair ramp at its front steps—that's diversity without inclusion.

On the other hand, inclusion without diversity fails to expand its traditional group members. It "includes" who is already likely to come—not unlike the typical scene of a country club, which tends to attract the kind of membership it already boasts. Knowing what inclusivity *isn't*—it isn't token diversity, and it isn't undemanding cultural sameness—starts to get us closer to what inclusivity *is*.

Throughout Peter's story and in the illustrations above, the three qualifying features of inclusivity have been introduced: to be inclusive is to be welcoming, supportive, and respectful. And full, meaningful participation—no matter an organization's activities—is integral to the way welcome, support, and respect are communicated.

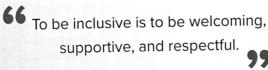

> **"** To be inclusive is to be welcoming, supportive, and respectful. **"**

And young people are clear: inclusivity is a priority for them, and it *should* be a priority for any organization that wants their participation. Peter's hope for inclusion at his university mirrors the high regard for this value among young people surveyed by Springtide. A majority of these young people, ages 13 to 25, say that the people and groups they associate with must demonstrate a sense of welcome, respect, and support; organizations must invite and enable full participation, regardless of individual differences.

About three-quarters (72%) of our respondents say it is important that the organizations they join create spaces where *everyone* is safe, welcome, and has equal access to resources. And more than 60% of the young people we surveyed agree that people should be treated equally no matter what it takes to do so—amounting to a concrete and serious demand for welcome, support, and respect.

72%

of young people surveyed say it is important that the organizations they join **create spaces where everyone is safe, welcome, and has equal access to resources.**

SPRINGTIDE™ NATIONAL RESEARCH RESULTS
© 2020 Springtide. Cite, share, and join the conversation at springtideresearch.org.

Nearly 40% say that they will join an organization *only* if it values inclusion among its highest priority. Our research indicates further that young people value inclusion with diversity. In fact, when considering their current or future workplaces, nearly half our respondents say they would choose to work for an organization that had high regard for diversity, even if it paid less. Lacking true inclusivity (diversity and inclusion) universities, workplaces, and other organizations, institutions, and spaces hold little appeal to young people.

In the examples that follow, it will become clear that diversity alone isn't good enough for young people. Instead, the practice of inclusivity—welcome, support, respect, and meaningful participation—is key for appealing to the sensibilities of young people.

DIVERSITY DOES NOT EQUAL INCLUSION

Whether at work, in school, or at worship; whether spending money, time, or social capital—organizations that are inclusive are organizations young people want to join. And as Peter's story illustrated in the opening of this chapter, an inclusive community is not one that admits or invites a diverse group of people to share time and space together while retaining a culture that caters to only one type of member. It's clear that inclusivity is *more* than token diversity.

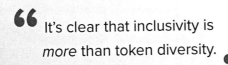

> 66 It's clear that inclusivity is *more* than token diversity. 99

Misunderstanding the subtle but significant distinctions among diversity, equity, and inclusion has consequences. A 2017 *Harvard Business Review* article, "Diversity Doesn't Stick without Inclusion," authors Laura Sherbin and Ripa Rashid argue that a major stumbling block for organizations—and particularly workplaces—that seek to demonstrate inclusivity as a value is that they instead conflate diversity with the value they mean to be practicing.

"Part of the problem is that 'diversity' and 'inclusion' are so often lumped together that they're assumed to be the same thing. But that's just not the case. In the workplace, diversity equals representation. Without inclusion, however, the crucial connections that attract diverse talent, encourage participation, foster innovation, and lead to business growth won't happen." Quoting diversity advocate Vernã Myers, the article states: "'Diversity is being invited to the party. Inclusion is being asked to dance.'"

"Numerous studies show that diversity alone doesn't drive inclusion," the article reports.

In a 2018 *Gallup: Workplace* article, Ella Washington and Camille Patrick make similar observations about the importance of fostering a diverse *and* inclusive culture within an organization, and the critical difference between these two qualities: "Gallup's research indicates recognizing that diversity and inclusion are very different things is the first step in the journey toward creating a uniquely diverse and inclusive culture."

Over 60%

of the young people we surveyed agree that **people should be treated equally no matter what** it takes to do so.

Washington and Patrick note that diversity can be assessed with quantitative measures, but that assessing inclusion requires a more nuanced approach: "Inclusion refers to a cultural and environmental feeling of belonging. It can be assessed as the extent to which employees are valued, respected, accepted, and encouraged to fully participate in the organization. Employees in inclusive environments feel appreciated for their unique characteristics and are therefore comfortable sharing their ideas and other aspects of their true and authentic selves."

As a means of self-assessment, organizations must "define what diversity means for their unique culture and how they expect inclusion to manifest on their teams. Next, they must have objective data to indicate if they *are* diverse and inclusive," according to Washington and Patrick.

Given that nearly 40% of the young people Springtide surveyed agreed an organization *must* hold inclusivity as one of its highest values, this kind of nuanced understanding is critical to getting it right. **Organizational leaders have a simple recipe for success in assessing behaviorally whether their organization is perceived and experienced as inclusive: just ask members.** Ask members if their experiences and opinions are solicited, received with respect, and acted on. Ask if they feel respected and valued for their strengths, and if organizational leaders are perceived as trustworthy to do what's right when issues arise. The answers to such questions will reveal whether inclusivity is an organizational strength.

ACT > ON THE DATA: Want to know if the young people you serve feel valued, respected, accepted, and encouraged to fully participate? Ask them. Then be responsive to what you hear.

CREATING A WELCOMING, SUPPORTIVE, RESPECTFUL, PARTICIPATIVE ENVIRONMENT

The primary measure of inclusivity is whether an organization or group conveys a sense of welcome, respect, support, and valued participation. By that measure, Radiant City Arts, an organization that provides arts education, is creating inclusive spaces for young people. Cofounded by artist-educators Akili Jackson, Benjamin Cohen, and Yusuf Abdul Lateef, Radiant City specializes in music, poetry, and visual arts workshops, "with a focus on developing leadership skills and self-empowerment," according to its website. Working with students throughout Michigan and Ohio, Radiant City has engaged in education projects with public, private, and charter schools and has worked with library systems, after-school programs, and youth detention and rehabilitation centers.

At the invitation of Salem Lutheran pastor Michael Hanck, visual artist Lateef and musician Cohen led a vocational exploration for high school students from the North End neighborhood of Toledo. The exploration included an art tour that gave students a chance to engage in screen printing, painting, sculpture, bookbinding, sound design, songwriting, beat-making, and recording studio technology. "With each learned skill, students are exposed to a different creative path and potential career direction," Lateef told *Toledo City Paper*. At the end of the exploration, the teens' art was displayed in a Toledo gallery in an exhibit titled "Hear. I Am."

The title emerged from the interfaith dialogue that arose between Lateef, a Muslim, and the teens, who were associated with Salem Lutheran. Pastor Hanck commented on the inclusive nature of the exhibit title in an interview with *Living Lutheran* magazine. "['Hear. I Am.'] invokes the divine name—a common one that we can all share, and which, for me, invokes the idea of the *imago Dei*, our being created in God's image. It's a very affirming and empowering title, 'Hear. I Am.' It's the cry of all human beings and of God's own self—a nonexclusive image."

Lateef echoed that understanding. "I see Allah's oneness when I allow myself to be open to people. The 'Hear. I Am.' project helped people realize the importance of art in society, which, in turn, helped folks see our true value in the overall mission of peace."

Hanck said the sense of inclusion the project inspires radiates to the surrounding community as well. "This is an area of town that often feels forgotten. But in this [project], we feel cared about. We feel warmth. We feel wanted." Inclusivity, in this example, is embodied in many ways: in the welcoming attitude of the founders at Radiant City Arts, in the support they give to students, in the respect shown between and among various faith traditions, and in the fundamental goal to invite young people to participate expansively in the arts.

The arts, in particular, provide a powerful opportunity for any organization to practice inclusivity, as music, literature, painting, theater, and so on. can be experienced and expressed by all people, regardless of skill level, socioeconomic status, religious and cultural background, etc. Beauty is, in this sense, naturally and profoundly inclusive. But the arts are not the only means for practicing inclusivity; plenty of other organizations and individuals demonstrate this value in meaningful, notable ways. And this matters, as 72% of our respondents say it is important that the organizations to which they belong work to create spaces where everyone is safe, welcome, and equally resourced.

66 The arts, in particular, provide a powerful opportunity for any organization to practice inclusivity, as music, literature, painting, theater, and so on. can be experienced and expressed by all people, regardless of skill level, socioeconomic status, religious and cultural background, etc. Beauty is, in this sense, naturally and profoundly inclusive. **99**

 ACT ⟩ ON THE DATA: You don't have to be an arts organization to take advantage of the way art can help you practice inclusivity. Host a film night or post a poem (not a controversial news article!) on your organization's social media channels. Invite a generative conversation—one that welcomes, supports, and respects the full participation (opinions, ideas, and sentiments included) of all members.

CREATIVITY IS KEY FOR PRACTICING INCLUSION

Religious organizations have a reputation—whether earned or unfair—for conveying a distinct sense of exclusivity. When to sit, stand, kneel, bow; what words to sing and when to sing them: it makes sense that these rituals, without explanation or *with* accompanying judgment or lack of welcome, would give this impression. The irony is that for many churches, mosques, synagogues, and other places of worship, this is precisely the opposite of what they hope to communicate. Many, in theory, really want to practice inclusivity—they just don't know how.

Perhaps it's no surprise, then, that young people are leaving or simply never becoming involved in religious communities in the first place. **If a place refuses to embrace or show respect for those who seem not to conform to a more traditional set of practices or appearances, young people will connect with their sense of the sacred someplace else.**

A research organization within the Muslim community in the United States offers some valuable insight into what young Muslims most value in their places of worship. Inclusivity is high on the list. In the study "Reimagining Muslim Spaces," the Institute for Social Policy and Understanding (ISPU) conducted a case study of the Muslim community MakeSpace, a self-identified Muslim third space[1] in Washington, DC.

MakeSpace describes itself on its Facebook page as "an inclusive, welcoming, and relevant hub for the Washington Metropolitan area Muslim community, with a strong focus on youth and young professionals."

---

[1] *Third space* refers to a public space or community where people find meaningful connections and experience belonging. One's home is a first space, and one's school or work is a second space.

As part of the ISPU study, an opinion survey was conducted on the motivation of MakeSpace participants. Topping the list of major attractors for young people to MakeSpace are a welcoming atmosphere (83% agreement) and diversity of age and ethnicity (72%)—both key factors for creating an inclusive space.

One 24-year-old female survey respondent said that young people are particularly vulnerable to feelings of criticism or judgment that they may experience in a traditional mosque community. At MakeSpace, she explained, an atmosphere of nonjudgmental welcome pervades.

"Even if you have the *niyah* [explicit intention made before an act] of doing something for the sake of Allah, that goes away because of the negative energy and the feeling of being invalid or insufficient, which is something that really should be between a person and God. For youth specifically, [who] are naturally self-conscious and insecure, when you enter a space that is critical of how you're worshipping, something as intimate as that, it can be crushing. [At] MakeSpace whenever you go to prayer . . . people are smiling and they're happy and you feel adequate. You feel like you belong in that space. You don't have people actively judging you."

Her response captures many hallmarks of inclusivity, and makes sense of the popularity of MakeSpace among young Muslims in the DC area. A sense of welcome that helps a person overcome self-consciousness, a sense of support during an intimate and vulnerable act of prayer, a sense of respect and reverence pervading the worship space—all these factors combine to make full and meaningful participation *possible*. Reimagining the mosque, while still keeping its central tenets and commitments, turned a judgmental-feeling space into one of great inclusivity.

Becoming a more inclusive environment doesn't necessarily mean starting from scratch. It means creatively reimagining how welcome, support, and respect can look while keeping an organization's key identity and purpose intact. This work is

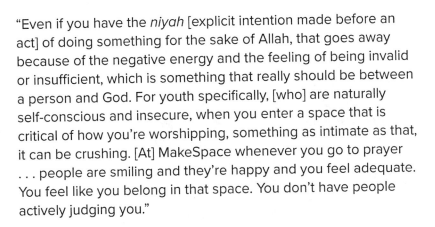

difficult, but necessary. And it often begins with listening to the needs of those young people who may explicitly feel unwelcome, unsupported, or disrespected.

ACT ⟩ **ON THE DATA:** To create a more inclusive environment, begin by listening to the needs of those young people who feel unwelcome, unsupported, or disrespected.

SEEKING INCLUSIVE SPACES

When Peter arrived at the Ivy League institution he'd hoped to attend, his expectations and his lived experience were incongruent. Though he was admitted to the university, he didn't feel a sense of welcome, support, respect, or opportunity for full participation in campus life, given his socioeconomic background and the worldview forged from it. The campus was practicing diversity without inclusion—it invited him to their community but didn't do what it took to make sure he felt he belonged there.

As reported earlier in this chapter, nearly 40% of young people surveyed by Springtide say they will join an institution only if it values inclusion as its highest priority. And more than 60% say that people should be treated equally no matter what it takes to do so. Peter could very well have decided the uphill battle to belong at this school wasn't worth it; instead, he sought out spaces where he was likely to find support and camaraderie.

Since Peter wasn't finding like-minded peers on campus, he looked elsewhere. During his second year, he began working as a translator for a legal aid bureau. Concerned that local land-lords had unethical practices of "illegally evict[ing] non-English speaking tenants," Peter wanted to help. "The language barrier and inability to pay attorney fees is the biggest deterrent for people who have been illegally evicted," he explained.

Peter took pride in his work as a translator at the bureau. "I was honored to help those left behind by our . . . judicial system. I understood their situation to an extent. I could just as easily have been in that situation, and I wanted to play a part in fixing the broken system that leaves poor immigrants" behind.

By showing up to spaces that were inherently inclusive—a legal aid clinic demonstrating support, welcome, and respect for volunteers *and* those in need of legal help, encouraging and even empowering participation in the judicial system—Peter started to feel more comfortable. But even more important, he found a community of like-minded peers he couldn't find on campus. Other classmates were also volunteering at the legal aid bureau. "That is how I met most of my friends," he remarked. "Turns out, there were other people like me on campus. They were just few and far between. We had similar stories: under-privileged kids who understood how unfair life can be. We wanted to prevent harm in any way we could."

Peter explained: "They knew how hard being poor is; they also wanted to help disenfranchised communities. Not only did I meet people who were empathetic when I couldn't afford an $8 cocktail, they were also empathetic of my lifelong goals. . . . They wanted to start nonprofits, become local politicians to help their communities, or work for a civil rights law firm."

Though the campus itself didn't formally usher Peter into the relationships that ended up creating the sense of welcome, respect, and support he craved, this story is still a happy one. And it reveals one of the most significant facets of the way this value drives young people: If an organization *isn't* practicing inclusivity, young people won't settle for token diversity or put up with undemanding cultural sameness in a group they join. Not unlike the way young people expect organizations to do *whatever it takes* to practice inclusivity, they themselves will do what it takes. They will, as Peter's case shows us, pursue this value with creativity, energy, and open-mindedness until welcome, support, respect, and full participation are embraced and experienced by everyone in the group.

> **66** Not unlike the way that young people expect organizations to do *whatever it takes* to practice inclusivity, they themselves will do what it takes. **99**

BRINGING IT ALL TOGETHER

Takeaways

1. To be inclusive is to be welcoming, supportive, and respectful. And full, meaningful participation—no matter an organization's activities—is integral to the way welcome, support, and respect is communicated.

2. Young people are clear: inclusivity is a priority for them, and it *should* be a priority for any organization that wants their participation.

3. An inclusive community is not one that just admits or invites a diverse group of people to share time and space together and nonetheless retains a culture that only caters to one type of member. It's clear that inclusivity is *more* than token diversity.

4. The difference between diversity and inclusion is important to get right. Organizational leaders have a simple recipe for success in assessing behaviorally whether their organization is perceived and experienced as inclusive: just ask members.

5. The arts provide a powerful opportunity for any organization to practice inclusivity, as music, literature, painting, theater, and so on. can be experienced and expressed by all people, regardless of skill level, socioeconomic status, religious and cultural background, etc. Beauty is, in this sense, naturally and profoundly inclusive.

6. If a place refuses to embrace or show respect for those who seem not to conform to a more traditional set of practices or appearances, young people will connect their sense of the sacred someplace else.

7. Not unlike the way young people expect organizations to do *whatever it takes* to practice inclusivity, they themselves will do what it takes.

✓ Act on the Data

❑ Want to know if the young people you serve feel valued, respected, accepted, and encouraged to fully participate? Ask them. Then be responsive to what you hear.

❑ You don't have to be an arts organization to take advantage of the way art can help you practice inclusivity. Host a film night or post a poem (not a controversial news article!) on your organization's social media channels. Invite a generative conversation—one that welcomes, supports, and respects the full participation (opinions, ideas, and sentiments included) of all members.

❑ To create a more inclusive environment, begin by listening to the needs of those young people who feel unwelcome, unsupported, or disrespected.

❑ Pay attention to the groups of people who *aren't* showing up. Reach out to them to find out why.

Reflect on Your Experience

- Can you call to mind an organization—perhaps yours—that practices diversity without inclusion? What about inclusion without diversity? Spend time thinking about the nuance between these two values and how they look when embodied—or not—in various institutions. What would it look like if true inclusivity were practiced?

- Young people make it clear that organizations should do whatever it takes to practice inclusivity and to equip members of their group to fully participate. With boundless resources, what would the ideal version of this look like in your organization?

REFERENCES

Emily, Sarah. "A Brilliant Presence." *Toledo City Paper,* June 19, 2019.

Kapila, Monisha, Ericka Hines, and Martha Searby. "Why Diversity, Equity, and Inclusion Matter." Independent Sector website, October 6, 2016.

Kaplan, Phillip L. "Art Worker: Yusuf Lateef." *The Blade,* May 14, 2019.

Mahmood, Faiqa. "Understanding Inclusivity Practices at 'Third Spaces' | MakeSpace: A Case Study." Institute for Social Policy and Understanding, September 17, 2016.

Saunders, Jay. "Mission-Driven Art: Ohio Congregation Gives Youth Spiritual, Creative Outlet." *Living Lutheran* volume 4, no. 7, November 2019: 17–19.

Sherbin, Laura, and Ripa Rashid. "Diversity Doesn't Stick without Inclusion." *Harvard Business Review,* February 1, 2017.

Washington, Ella, and Camille Patrick. "3 Requirements for a Diverse and Inclusive Culture." *Gallup: Workplace,* September 17, 2018.

CHAPTER 3

AUTHENTIC

"Belonging is wherever I don't feel judged," says Sarah. "It's wherever I can have a conversation with someone and they are vulnerable. I'm used to being vulnerable, so I like people who are vulnerable too."

Another word for *vulnerable* is *unguarded*. What Sarah describes in these relationships is not about revealing intimate details or taking risks with personal sharing—it is about the ability to feel safe in that relationship without facade, pretense, or agenda. It's the ability to be fully and totally yourself; it is, in other words, the ability to be authentic.

Homeschooled through high school, Sarah had these kinds of deep relationships with family members and a next-door neighbor who was her same age. With these people, Sarah felt she could be her full self and expect the same in return. But finding that level of vulnerability outside her home context had always been a challenge for Sarah, a self-described introvert.

As part of her curriculum, Sarah attended weekly co-op meetings for other homeschooled students. Though she had peers there, she disliked the dynamics of these meetings. "Cliques formed, and I was left out. They would always gossip and use it as a way to keep people from joining their group," Sarah remarked. She described feeling alienated: "I couldn't relate to any of my peers. I wondered if there was something wrong with me."

Gossip proved an obstacle to authenticity—and understandably so. Conversations about others, especially malicious or maligning as gossip often is, are mechanisms to protect against and avoid vulnerability. Rather than authentically sharing, these students put barriers up that had the intended result: to exclude.

"I'm already shy, so I didn't try to build relationships. It was hard talking to people and ten times harder since I wanted to get away from the stereotypical gossip." Sarah believed her situation was made worse by being homeschooled, given her more limited circle for socializing. "Where does a sheltered homeschooled kid go to find genuine friends? I felt hopeless."

Although she didn't have many options for new or different peers during high school, at age 18, Sarah packed her bags for college. She had typical new-school nerves, with the added stress of having no previous public education experience. "I was so anxious. I didn't fit in with my homeschooled peers, and I assumed it would happen again in college." Despite these nerves, Sarah brought with her the hope of authentic relationships, like the ones she'd known from home but lacked among a wider group of peers.

But before we learn more about where Sarah did—and *didn't*—find these kinds of relationships, the chapter unpacks the term *authentic* and explores the high regard young people place on this value today.

AUTHENTICITY
Insights from Springtide Research

When Springtide surveyed young people about their values, we found that the desire for authenticity was widely shared among our respondents. In other words, Sarah is a case in point and not an exception. Authenticity is characterized by the ability to be totally oneself, to be completely genuine without worrying about performing a certain way—whether that means looking, acting, or speaking in some prescribed manner. With authenticity, consistency is key, as acting one way with some people and another with others comes off as insincere.

> **❝** Authenticity is characterized by the ability to be totally oneself, to be completely genuine without worrying about performing a certain way—whether that means looking, acting, or speaking in some prescribed manner. **❞**

This value is closely related to creativity, another highly regarded attribute among young people. And the connection makes sense: creativity is about originality, about seeing differently; it's about a unique perspective, a unique performance, or a unique person. Creativity gets at the heart of who a person is and how they express themselves. In this sense, **creativity is an outlet for authenticity—it's the ability to do something unexpected or unconventional, something original, without feeling the need to toe the party line or do what's been done before**.

Springtide findings show that nearly half our survey respondents (47%) feel that if they are not openly being who they truly are, they are lying to the world. Fifty-five percent of respondents agree that it is important to be their authentic selves when participating in an organization, and slightly more than half (51%) agree that people should get to be exactly who they are at work. In other words, young people see a tight connection between authenticity and honesty. If an organization wants honest, engaged volunteers, participants, or employees, then it needs to create an atmosphere where people can be authentic.

Fifty-five percent of respondents agree that it is **important to be their authentic selves when participating in an organization.**

SPRINGTIDE™ NATIONAL RESEARCH RESULTS
© 2020 Springtide. Cite, share, and join the conversation at springtideresearch.org.

Our research also shows that young people value creativity and imagination, those interconnected aspects of authenticity. Nearly 60% of those we surveyed agree that it's important for them to think of new ideas and be creative in order to do things their own way, and more than 70% say that it is important to intentionally allow time and space to activate the imagination.

It's clear that young people hold authenticity—and the cultivation of authenticity through creativity and imagination—in high regard. They not only want to live this value themselves, but they also want to participate in organizations that hold it in high esteem. This chapter offers examples of different groups that embody this value and that can serve as models for thinking about practicing authenticity amid other contexts as well.

HONESTY, AUTHORITY, AND AUTHENTICITY

Valuing authenticity so highly—with over 50% of young people agreeing that a person should be totally themselves, even at work—means that younger generations might behave by different social norms than older colleagues do. This is understandable, as millennials, Gen Z, and younger generations have been shaped by a different set of social conventions, many of which contribute to the high regard for authenticity over expected or routine interactions.

In a 2019 article from the Wharton School of Business at the University of Pennsylvania, Professor Stephanie Creary argues that young people today bring a "different set of social conventions" to the workplace. These can show up in communications and relationships, where young people sometimes demonstrate a level of honesty that is out of the norm—and sometimes difficult—for their older colleagues.

"Many older workers were trained to have a different relationship with people in positions of authority, such that we would address them much more formally," says Creary. "We were trained with the idea that regard for authority was really important regardless of whether you respected their ideas. This generation expects a much closer relationship with people of authority, so they can treat people who are higher in the hierarchy as their friend, and that can become a problem in a workplace where there are structures and chains of command that are important."

This difference in expected behavior is directly related to a high esteem for authenticity and creativity. Understanding hierarchy as a structure that prescribes particular ways of relating to one another, many young people find it an obstacle to more authentic interactions. It's less about bucking authority per se, and more about the tearing down of walls that prevent authenticity and creativity.

Creary's advice for intergenerational workplaces? Invite managers to have an in-person conversation with young workers, clarifying workplace norms and policies, and reinforcing them when necessary. But managers and supervisors should also give a little. Creary recommends getting to know younger workers on a more personal level. "Everyone has different levels of comfort around disclosing personal information," Creary acknowledges. "However, your Gen Z employee might be more inclined to share personal information as a way of creating a closer relationship with you. No one is asking you to share information that makes you feel uncomfortable, but consider whether there are any hobbies, fun facts, experiences, etc. that you can share with them that will help them to view you as a real person."

These principles and suggestions don't just apply to workplace settings or manager-employee relationships. Adopting a culture of authenticity is integral to helping young people succeed in whatever organization they're participating in, and small gestures—like more candid conversations—can go a long way. This helps prevent the impression that people have a "home" self and a "work" self, a split that feels dishonest and inauthentic to young people.

> **66** Adopting a culture of authenticity is integral to helping young people succeed in whatever organization they're participating in. **99**

If authenticity and creativity are about inviting a person's whole self to be not only permitted but explicitly *invited* into a relationship, any organization can adopt practices to further this goal. Whether gathering for work, school, worship, or anything else, any organization can begin practicing authenticity by encouraging personal sharing—as appropriate—among participants.

ACT ⟩ **ON THE DATA:** Especially if you lead young people in the context of an intergenerational setting, try to understand the social context, upbringing, and expectations of the young people you serve. Allow yourself to be a little vulnerable, and maybe encourage other older members to do the same. It might be difficult, but authenticity is not just for young people: it's a value that when practiced by many can encourage deeper understanding, empathy, and connection.

ADMIRING AND EXPRESSING AUTHENTICITY

Role Models and Influencers

In some circles, *authenticity* is a buzzword. In the world of social media, it gets tossed around as a response to the filtered photos, preset backgrounds, undisclosed paid promotions, and other tricks that give the impression a person's life is better, happier, or more adventurous than it really is. What can authenticity look like, especially in the context of relationships mediated through websites and apps?

A 2018 CNBC report asked young people about authenticity, and that survey—of women and girls ages 13–24—is largely consistent with Springtide findings on the same question, with a majority in the CNBC study confirming that "being true to their values and beliefs makes a person cool." The article in which these statistics are reported goes on: "But they're not so keen on celebrities: only 19 percent admire something or someone because they have a mass following." Traditional celebrities, like Hollywood movie stars or pop musicians, retain a powerful status among several generations, but many young people are put off by what they perceive as impersonal and scripted personas among many celebrities.

One 16-year-old young woman interviewed for the CNBC report explained, "Whereas someone like Selena Gomez clearly has a team of people polishing her image and making her life look perfect, online personalities are allowed to be candid about their personal issues, making them a lot more relatable." An "online celebrity" might be an average teenager with a great sense of humor on YouTube or stellar dance moves on TikTok. The point is, social media gives a chance to all people—celebrity actor, aspiring dog walker, local band teacher, or grandmother of two—to express themselves with creativity and originality, and to be "liked" by others for those reasons.

While filters (and other ways of masking what's real) can muddle this value, social media is essentially a neutral platform that can either facilitate true and authentic sharing or avoid it. As we know from our research, young people are eager to do the former. And what other generations might think is a form of vanity—things like posting selfies or writing long captions about one's inner feelings or struggles—is really a generational embrace of authenticity.

In fact, when it comes to selfies, young people are more likely to seize the opportunity for *realness*, "posting less-than-flattering selfies and relying on sassy picture captions over posed pictures and emojis." It's a way of practicing the value of authenticity and creativity, beginning with the very way young people put them- selves out into the world—literally. Rather than an act of vanity (or *mere* vanity), it's a subtle but powerful rejection of anything too pretty, too shiny, or too filtered, that is, anything that smacks of being inauthentic.

The importance of being real—including the emphasis on hon- esty from the previous example and the unfiltered, unscripted kinds of interactions in this example—is something young people want to not only practice themselves but also see modeled and embraced by those with influence of any kind. Young people know that authenticity invites authenticity. When one person starts to take down their walls, it encourages others to do the same.

> 66 Authenticity invites authenticity. When one person starts to take down their walls, it encourages others to do the same. 99

Social media is predicated on the way these trends, including the trend of sharing authentically, can catch fire and travel the internet. But the dynamics at work in these spaces provide valuable lessons for other contexts too. As a web of relationships amid strangers and friends, family and colleagues, deep connections and fleeting acquaintances, social media reflects the kinds of connections that already exist in the world. And the demand for authenticity in *all* these types of relationships is more than a buzzword. It's a real invitation to take seriously the chance for sincere self-expression—whether in selfies or staff meetings—and by extension, to permit others to do the same.

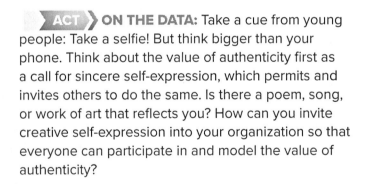

ACT ⟩ **ON THE DATA:** Take a cue from young people: Take a selfie! But think bigger than your phone. Think about the value of authenticity first as a call for sincere self-expression, which permits and invites others to do the same. Is there a poem, song, or work of art that reflects you? How can you invite creative self-expression into your organization so that everyone can participate in and model the value of authenticity?

Encouraging Creativity

Creativity can be a channel for authenticity, as it encourages a person to be original and unexpected in their interactions, ideas, and processes. It's no surprise that both creativity and authenticity—distinct but interrelated values—are highly valued by young people. Fifty-eight percent of young people Springtide surveyed agree that it's important for them to think up new ideas and be creative in order to do things their way. A striking 71% say that it is important to make intentional time and space to activate the imagination. Finding ways to incorporate opportunities for creativity in an organization is key to encouraging authenticity and, consequently, to creating a space that's attractive to young people.

71%

of young people in our survey say it is important to make **intentional time and space to activate the imagination.**

SPRINGTIDE™ NATIONAL RESEARCH RESULTS
© 2020 Springtide. Cite, share, and join the conversation at springtideresearch.org.

Perhaps the most famously creative workspace today is IDEO, a design and innovation lab based in California. Founded by David Kelly, the organization excels in creative problem-solving for all kinds of clients with all kinds of concerns. They invented the computer "mouse" and reinvented the shopping cart—and plenty in between.

The first two principles outlining their values and commitments as a company are explicitly about creativity. First, "Everyone is creative," and second, "Creative organizations are more flexible." Rather than relegating creativity to the domain of artists, IDEO insists that everyone's unique perspective is precisely what can and should be brought to a brainstorming session or a problem-solving meeting.

Writing for IDEO's blog in 2020 about the best piece of advice she received, Natalie Osterweil, a young woman in her thirties, explained that the value of realizing her unique perspective was precisely the way she could best serve her organization.

> **Early in my time here, I was on a walk with another organization-al designer, mid-existential crisis when she said to me, "Your job is to be thinking about what no one else in the room is thinking**

about." She helped me see that I didn't have to immediately have every answer or every iota of expertise; I just needed to be using my lens on the world to make our collective design richer.

Natalie's ability to feel comfortable in her role was directly related to accepting and embracing the call to creativity. And she could live more authentically when she realized she didn't need to perform creativity in some scripted way to keep up with her colleagues. Instead, she could just be herself. "Unlocking my creative process has been so much about believing in the value of what I bring to the table and understanding its unique contribution to what we are all building together." As previously noted, acting authentically and creatively in one's own life invites and encourages others to feel safe doing the same.

Opportunities for creativity can be hard to come up with for an organization with a fairly rigid or regular way of doing things. IDEO, among many other brands and consultants, offers some tools to get started breaking out of norms and accessing the creativity every person has and every organization needs. Some suggestions, from IDEO's blog "10 Exercises to Build Your Creative Confidence," include mind maps, empathy exercises, eliminating hierarchy for certain types of gatherings, and prototyping. **Any action an organization takes to start practicing creativity—and thereby authenticity—is a step in a proactive and powerful direction.** These types of opportunities for imagination are incredibly important. Not only will a culture of creativity appeal to young people, but it will also solidify the dynamism of any organization.

ACT ON THE DATA: Review the list of creativity-boosting exercises from IDEO or from another workbook or consultant you know. Decide to implement or test one new idea, even for a brief time, at regular intervals, whether every week, month, or quarter. Be sure to include a variety of group members in the exercises each time.

Authenticity Invites Authenticity

With her high regard for authenticity and her experience of a handful of relationships that modeled it (and a handful that didn't), Sarah began seeking relationships outside her home-school community.

Though she was worried she wouldn't find or be able to make friends who shared her desire for authenticity, Sarah was pleasantly surprised to find that "there's more space for people to be themselves" after high school; "I feel like I can be myself and my peers can do the same."

Sarah speculated why this might be. It could be a simple matter of maturity and age, or that educational spaces, in particular, are designed to help a young person consider new ideas, new ways of seeing the world—a recipe for authenticity and encounter. "Or maybe it's because everyone is also trying to make friends. We're all in the same boat. We have no preconceptions about each other. Everyone is lost and hoping to find their people. It has been easier to find genuinely good people."

Starting a new job, taking classes at a new school, or joining a new organization can provide an opportunity for a blank slate—facades, agendas, and pretenses come down while individuals decide who and how they want to be. It's an environment that encourages authenticity, even if it doesn't force it.

The gossip Sarah dreaded among high school peers is non-existent with her new friends, she says. "We don't even think about talking down to other people. It doesn't even cross our minds. I love it because being so negative seems pointless to me. I'd much rather talk about class or our weekend plans." Sarah found a group of friends who valued straightforward conversations about real things, rather than the unoriginal and inauthentic discussion of others.

Once embarrassed by her quiet reserve, Sarah feels well accepted and able to open up among her new friends. "A lot of my new friends understood that I was a quiet person and gave me time to warm up to them," she told us. "They are like introvert whisperers. They give me time to respond during conversations. They notice if I'm being left out of the conversation and rope me back in. They aren't trying to change me either. They accept me for who I am." These peers embodied a kind of authenticity that made space for Sarah to be fully herself.

The freedom of feeling fully herself is expansive, creative. Though at the time of this conversation Sarah hadn't yet joined any new clubs or sports, she remarked that—even as a self-proclaimed introvert—she was interested in getting involved in things "like photography and art." Content with the status of her friendships, she is eager for creative pursuits that stretch her out of her comfort zone in other ways, but, she says, "If I made one or two more close friends, I wouldn't complain."

Sarah was able to be totally herself with her new group of friends after leaving the more socially constricted and inauthentic relationships from her homeschool community. The freedom and safety of authenticity means more room for continued self-expression and self-expansion through creative outlets. Like Sarah, a young person in any organization will almost certainly thrive and grow in a setting where authenticity is the norm and creativity is encouraged.

Bringing It All Together

Takeaways

1. Creativity gets at the heart of who a person is and how they express themselves. In this sense, creativity is an outlet for authenticity—it's the ability to do something unexpected or unconventional, something original, without feeling the need to toe the party line or do what's been done before.

2. Adopting a culture of authenticity is integral to helping young people succeed in whatever organization they're participating in, and small gestures—like more candid conversations—can go a long way.

3. The importance of being real is something young people want to not only practice themselves but also see modeled and embraced by those with influence of any kind. Young people know that authenticity invites authenticity. When one person starts to take down their walls, it encourages others to do the same.

4. Any action an organization takes to start practicing creativity—and thereby authenticity—is a step in a proactive and powerful direction. These types of opportunities for imagination are incredibly important. Not only will a culture of creativity appeal to young people, but it will also solidify the dynamism of any organization.

✓ Act on the Data

❑ Especially if you lead young people in the context of an intergenerational setting, try to understand the social context, upbringing, and expectations of the young people you serve. Allow yourself to be a little vulnerable, and maybe encourage other older members to do the same. It might be difficult, but authenticity is not just for young people. It's a value that when practiced by many can encourage deeper understanding, empathy, and connection.

❑ Take a cue from young people: Take a selfie! But think bigger than your phone. Think about the value of authenticity first as a call for sincere self-expression, which permits and invites others to do the same. Is there a poem, song, or work of art that reflects you? How can you invite creative self-expression into your organization so that everyone can participate in and model the value of authenticity?

□ Review the list of creativity-boosting exercises from IDEO or from another workbook or consultant you know. Decide to implement or test one new idea, even for a brief time, at regular intervals, whether every week, month, or quarter. Be sure to include a variety of group members in the exercises each time.

Reflect on Your Experience

- What contexts come to mind when thinking of the term *authentic*? In what ways does your organization already embody this value, and in what ways could it improve?

- Taking seriously the idea that everyone is inherently creative, how can your organization begin to foster opportunities for individuals to exercise their creative muscles—and in so doing, begin creating a culture of authenticity?

REFERENCES

Cottong, Ali. "IDEO Designers Share the Best Creative Advice They've Ever Received." IDEO blog, February 28, 2020.

Handley, Lisa. "There's a Generation below Millennials and Here's What They Want from Brands." CNBC website, April 16, 2018.

"Make Way for Generation Z in the Workplace," January 22, 2019, from the website of Wharton School of Business at the University of Pennsylvania.

Perry, Saige. "10 Exercises to Build Your Creative Confidence." IDEO blog, August 22, 2019.

CHAPTER 4

WELCOMING

At age 22, Cheryl was wandering around New York City, but not aimlessly. She wasn't adrift in the chaos and crowds of the city, but she was searching for something—though she didn't know quite where to look or just when she'd find it.

As a volunteer missionary with her church—the Evangelical Lutheran Church of America (ELCA)—Cheryl and a close friend moved to New York with a sense of purpose. Her experiences and upbringing in the ELCA were positive, warm, and helped to shape the trajectory of her life path in significant ways.

Writing on her blog around the time she moved there, Cheryl notes that her formation in the church included mission trips and mentoring from trusted adults, as well as opportunities for deep and lasting friendships. In the same post, she powerfully describes the way her home church in North Dakota "walked alongside me with selfless love when I lost my father."

Arriving in New York, Cheryl was looking for home. "The first two weeks we tried different churches," she wrote. Two "were nice and had air conditioning and comfortable seats. But neither were communities that I was counting the seconds before I could return. Neither offered a service that connected with my heart."

Searching for something intangible, like the felt experience of *home* in a new city, a church community to which she could commit and belong eagerly, Cheryl couldn't exactly describe why the first two churches weren't quite right.

Eager to find a new church home but anxious that the wrong culture could sour her positive impressions of the spiritual community that had meant so much to her, Cheryl treaded lightly. The third week, she attended a church for the sole reason of it being relatively nearby, as she was crunched for time. She describes the experience:

> **Drudgingly I went. I struggle because whenever I walk into the doors of an ELCA congregation, I have this deep fear that this congregation will ruin my love of the ELCA by not being welcoming or by not living out the values that I know to be important. I grew up as a devout ELCA Lutheran youth, and my home congregation shaped so much of who I am that I would be devastated to experience other ELCA churches that were not doing the same for their youth.**

She knew what she was seeking: a church that was warm and inviting, that greeted her when she arrived and made her feel she belonged.

Whether in rural North Dakota or the urban neighborhoods of Brooklyn, whether in religious or secular spaces where they volunteer, work, or play, young people are seeking this hard-to-describe experience in the spaces at which they show up. An invitation to participate, a sense of belonging, a warm greeting—they are looking for an experience of *welcome*. In this chapter, we unpack what the value of being welcoming is, what our data tell us about how young people feel about this value, and how it can look in a variety of contexts.

WELCOMING
Insights from Springtide Research

The value of *welcoming* is unlike other values in this book, as it can describe two things. First, it can refer to the gestures of hospitality that an organization or person enacts. Second, it can describe the felt experience of the individual who is joining a new community or organization. The practice of welcoming a person and the feeling of being welcomed go hand in hand. Taking time to learn about one inevitably sheds light on the other.

The felt experience of being welcomed is, as Cheryl's story illustrates, hard to describe. For each person, a sense of welcome will be a mix of subtle but significant gestures. Still, this value has broad hallmarks: to be welcomed is to be received warmly, greeted intentionally, and accepted without obstacle or condition upon arrival. Feeling welcomed, especially as a newcomer to a community or organization, means there is space prepared (emotionally, physically, spiritually, and so on). It gives the distinct impression that the group was awaiting and expecting the new person.

> **66** To be welcomed is to be received warmly, greeted intentionally, and accepted without obstacle or condition upon arrival. **99**

How is this experience created and cultivated by groups? Gestures of welcome—the other half of how we might define *welcoming*—are also diverse and numerous, but a few constants tend to arise when we discover organizations that embody this value. Welcoming a person into a new faith community, sports team, or workplace means greeting the person by name, making eye contact, showing immediate interest, and connecting that person to others in the group right away. It means encouraging large-group and individual relationships, and helping facilitate both. It means acknowledging the new person in a way that doesn't put them on the spot, but celebrates their presence and invites them into greater and greater participation over time.

This two-part definition may be hard to imagine in the abstract, but when embodied by different organizations, it becomes clear how powerful the value of welcoming really is.

Springtide research on this value shows that young people recognize its power and importance not only for the organizations they might join but also for themselves to practice and embody. Our findings show that nearly 60% of young people surveyed feel responsible for welcoming people in any and all contexts, and more than 70% of respondents say it is important that organizations they belong to create spaces where everyone is safe and welcome.

Nearly 60%

of young people surveyed feel responsible for **welcoming people in any and all contexts.**

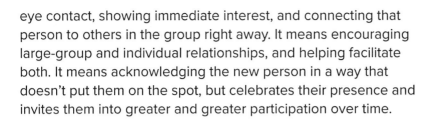

SPRINGTIDE™ NATIONAL RESEARCH RESULTS
© 2020 Springtide. Cite, share, and join the conversation at **springtideresearch.org.**

The inverse is true too: more than half (55%) say they will not remain engaged in an organization if they consistently feel like an outsider. And when asked about current or future workplaces, nearly 50% say that the employer is responsible for making employees feel welcome when they begin a new job. Young people expect that sense of welcome to happen right away, and to be facilitated thoughtfully by the community they're joining. If they don't feel this, they will leave.

Knowing how important the value of welcoming is for young people, we spend this chapter looking at organizations that create *an experience of welcoming by practicing welcoming gestures.* In other words, we take the two parts of this value and embody them with examples of how *welcoming* can look in a variety of contexts.

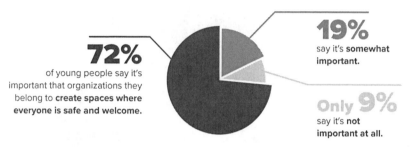

72% of young people say it's important that organizations they belong to **create spaces where everyone is safe and welcome.**

19% say it's **somewhat important.**

Only **9%** say it's **not important at all.**

SPRINGTIDE™ NATIONAL RESEARCH RESULTS
© 2020 Springtide. Cite, share, and join the conversation at **springtideresearch.org.**

ONBOARDING AND ORIENTATION AS WELCOMING PRACTICES

A majority of young people we surveyed expect to not only be welcomed—whether it be at a place of worship, a job setting, or some other group or organization—but also to be responsible for welcoming others. One company that goes out of its way to create a culture of welcome is Warby Parker, particularly in their well-honed practice of onboarding.

Commenting in an article for the online *First Round Review,* Warby Parker founders, Dave Gilboa and Neil Blumenthal, explained the importance the eyeglass manufacturer places on onboarding. "You have to make people feel special and welcome from the very first moment they interact with your organization," says Gilboa. Efforts include a unique welcome packet that includes an office map, a style guide, and a copy of Jack Kerouac's *Dharma Bums,* which inspired the company name. Gilboa said the intent is to make the company "heritage part of the employee experience from day one."

A helium balloon attached to a new employee's desk signals others in the company to go out of their way to extend welcome, and other onboarding efforts are driven by company leaders, in part because they possess institutional knowledge and also to drive home the importance of new employees to the company.

Warby Parker's attention to small but meaningful details—like a helium balloon, a map, and an invitation into the company's very identity with the gift of a book—combine to make sure the new person experiences welcome. **A new employee arrives with the unmistakable sense that their coworkers were expecting, even awaiting, their arrival. But perhaps even more important than these small gestures or orienting materials is that they always happen on day one.**

Nearly 50% of young people say that the employer is responsible for making employees feel welcome when they begin a new job.

55% say they **will not remain engaged** in an organization if they consistently feel like an outsider.

SPRINGTIDE™ NATIONAL RESEARCH RESULTS
© 2020 Springtide. Cite, share, and join the conversation at springtideresearch.org.

The significance of onboarding and welcoming someone right away cannot be overstated. It seals the first impression and heads off the inevitable worries and concerns that come with being new to a group or organization. "You feel like you have to prove your value right away," the *First Round Review* article observes. "Everyone around you has some degree of shared history, inside jokes, and institutional knowledge." While many of those cultural factors are reasons to *join* a company, they can also be off-putting to someone who isn't already well versed in it. This is why a thoughtful process of onboarding, of welcoming, matters so much.

This warm and thoughtful welcome at the start of a new job isn't just important for the new employee: it's important for the company. In an article for *Quartz at Work*, Liz Fosslien and Mollie West Duffy summarize a finding from a 2017 study of language in the workplace, "Alignment at Work," to offer a compelling case for a welcoming workplace. "Not belonging or feeling a sense of isolation is among the strongest predictors of turnover. A study analyzing emails showed new employees who do not switch from 'I' to 'we' pronouns during the first six months at their jobs are also more likely to leave."

In this case, Warby Parker not only welcomes new employees but also gives them the chance to share that positive experience and welcome others—a high value for young people. The popularity of the brand among young people is a reflection of this attentiveness to the experience of others.

Other organizations can learn from this example: welcoming a new person into a group, team, club, or company should be a thoughtful set of gestures and activities with goals to greet, give direction, and begin initiating that person in the culture, language, and history of the organization. When this warm welcome is offered by many within the organization and happens on the first day, it is even more powerful.

> **"** Welcoming a new person into a group, team, club, or company should be a thoughtful set of gestures and activities with goals to greet, give direction, and begin initiating that person in the culture, language, and history of the organization. **"**

ACT **ON THE DATA:** Imagine creating a "Welcoming Kit" for your organization. What would be included to help a new person understand your history or identity? How would that person's schedule help them get to know individuals and the whole group? Consider implementing a real welcome strategy, if you don't already have one, for both new members and those who may be on the periphery of joining. How might you welcome them in different ways?

CREATING EXPERIENCES OF SAFETY AND WELCOME–THREE EXAMPLES

More than 70% of Springtide survey respondents say it is important that organizations they belong to create spaces where everyone is safe and welcome. **The role of safety in creating a sense of welcome is an important one, as it is nearly impossible for a person to feel welcomed if they don't feel safe.** But more than that, if a person feels safe, they can participate more freely in the organization.

Providing Access for People with Special Needs

Safety is central to feeling welcome in many communities. People who are physically other-abled are unwelcome in many spaces, not for malicious reasons but to protect them from possible injury. But accessibility and full participation are integral to feeling welcome, so buildings or parks that *can't* provide safety to all members of a community fail to be truly welcoming.

Gordan and Maggie Hartman witnessed this firsthand, as their daughter with special needs was unwelcome at a hotel swimming pool on a family vacation. They resolved at that moment to find ways for their daughter—and others who may feel ex-cluded or unsafe in spaces built for the general public—to fully participate in the adventures of a theme park. In 2010, they built Morgan's Wonderland, "the world's first theme park designed with special-needs individuals in mind and built for everyone's enjoyment." Safety is the highest priority, followed closely by fun and play.

It is a beacon of welcome, explicitly inviting "everyone with a special need—young and older, healthy or ailing, introspective or outgoing," to a completely wheelchair-accessible park filled with "rides, playgrounds, and other colorful attractions." But those with special needs are not the only ones invited. In an interview with a local ABC station, Hartman describes the theme park as a place for "those who have special needs and those who don't have special needs to come together" and play in ways that neither person may have thought possible before.

To build a 25-acre theme park full of accessible, fun, and safe features for all people is a clear, resounding, and remarkable gesture of welcome.

Welcoming People of All Gender and Sexual Identities

Safety can mean many things. For LGBTQ+ individuals, this may look like gender-neutral bathrooms, a culture of explicitly asking about or naming preferred pronouns, or an official affirming stance in the public mission of an organization. But even simpler than that, an organization that supports and affirms all people regardless of gender or sexual identity can display a sign that reads "All Are Welcome."

An organization dedicated to the work of welcome, education, and advocacy, The Welcoming Project provides free yard or window signs with the colors of the rainbow that read, simply,

"All Are Welcome." As their website states, this is "to encourage businesses, health care/service providers, organizations, and congregations to display welcoming signs for the purpose of making LGBTQ . . . individuals and allies feel welcomed as patrons."

It's a simple gesture, but one that goes a long way to make clear that a certain space, group, club, or class is not hostile to their very identity.

Creating Safety in the School Cafeteria

At a school, efforts to prioritize safety may, again, look different. They may look like a series of programs aimed at dismantling a culture of bullying and creating a culture of connection, as in the case of We Dine Together.

Denis Estimon immigrated to the United States from Port-au-Prince, Haiti, when he was in the first grade. Unable to communicate with his classmates, Denis understood early on what it feels like to be isolated—and he didn't want that for others. That's why, during his senior year in high school in Boca Raton, Florida, Denis and his friends launched We Dine Together as an effort to combat the social isolation that can happen at school and, specifically, at the lunch table.

In the program, older students mentor and invite younger students, who are more vulnerable and prone to feeling excluded, unwelcome, or unsure where they belong, into the community by seeing that they do not eat alone at school. The older students help their mentees create relationships and gain confidence by responding to an often-unspoken anxiety around lunchroom cliques. We Dine Together provides a sense of welcome through the element of safety.

Today the program is national and part of the three-pronged Be Strong program (other prongs are a student rep program and a resilience program). Be Strong provides resources, support, and intervention for those who are affected by bullying, depression, or suicide, and teaches best practices on combating adversity through hope and resiliency training.

ACT ⟩ **ON THE DATA:** Safety makes it possible to feel welcome. What are things your community is already doing to cultivate a culture of safety for all members? Whether about individuals who identify as LGBTQ+, those with special needs, or young people in general, take something concrete—like your signage and website—and try to read it from an outsider's perspective. Does it tell a story of safety and welcome?

As the definition makes clear, to be welcomed is to be greeted, received, and accepted without obstacle or condition at arrival. But some communities and individuals regularly encounter these barriers to entry and marked experiences of unwelcome. In each of the previous examples, the experience of welcome is predicated on making sure a new person feels safe.

Safety is a way of communicating to someone that there is space for them; that an organization wouldn't just tolerate their presence, but celebrate it. This is why a truly welcoming organization is one that goes out of its way to create an environment that's safe for everyone—a value that young people overwhelmingly affirm is an important practice for any organization they join.

Welcome: The Beginning of Belonging

Young people enter relationships, groups, clubs, and organizations because of certain commonalities—shared interests, values, beliefs, practices, vocations, or professions. But they stay in those relationships when they feel like they belong.

The interview data from the Springtide report *Belonging: Reconnecting America's Loneliest Generation* show a clear pattern as young people move from joining a group to experiencing belonging within that group.

Over and over again, three distinct experiences show up in young people's stories: feeling noticed, feeling named, and feeling known. These experiences build on one another to deepen the overall experience of belonging. This movement can happen quickly or slowly. The word *feeling* in each instance doesn't refer to a fleeting emotional state or episode. It refers to a felt reality: a true, lasting, and concrete experience that invites and allows a relationship to flourish and deepen.

The value of being welcoming is integral to every stage of the process, which Springtide calls the Belongingness Process. To be welcoming is to notice someone on the periphery, invite them in by name, and ensure they are known and safe in your community.

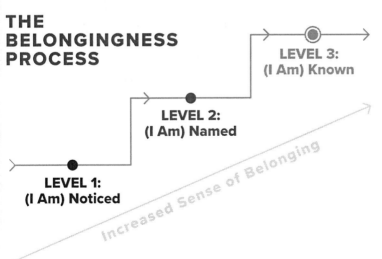

THE BELONGINGNESS PROCESS

LEVEL 3:
(I Am) Known

LEVEL 2:
(I Am) Named

LEVEL 1:
(I Am) Noticed

Increased Sense of Belonging

SPRINGTIDE™ NATIONAL RESEARCH RESULTS
© 2020 Springtide. Cite, share, and join the conversation at **springtideresearch.org**.
Original graphic from Belonging: Reconnecting America's Loneliest Generation
(Bloomington, MN: Springtide Research Institute, 2020), page 63.

ACT ❯❯ **ON THE DATA:** Practicing and implementing the Belongingness Process in your relationships with young people can be as simple as learning and using a person's name. When you first learn a young person's name, confirm that you are using their expressed pronouns and proper pronunciation. Memorize their name and use it three times in conversation soon after learning it, and again at every passing or gathering.

A Sense of Welcome, A Sense of Home

Cheryl begins a blog post about her experience at that third church she visited in her neighborhood: "I have something to share that I am so excited about that I can hardly contain it."

Though the church didn't have air conditioning, the incredible welcome Cheryl received quickly made up for any discomfort. "I was asked to put a name tag on, and greeted by Brent, a stay-at-home dad with two young girls. I noticed how small the sanctuary was, with maybe 50 chairs. Despite the size, I noticed people greeting each other, and I watched as the chairs filled, with almost no extras."

Throughout the service, Cheryl felt invited and encouraged: "The room was filled with powerful singing voices and a stunning organ," she recalled. Joining the music, rather than being a passive observer of a static community, she felt truly welcome, as a full participant. Combined with the greeting from Brent, the intentional practice of learning her name, and the intimacy of the setting, this church seized the chance to make a welcoming first impression.

The sermon given by the pastor resonated with and challenged Cheryl. People shook one another's hands at the sign of peace, a moment in the liturgy where the gathered community turns to one another to greet and bless one another. Cheryl writes, "Everyone shook EVERYONE'S hand. Everyone greeted one another with genuine smiles." It was clear even at a glance that this community had a culture of warmth and welcome that didn't just extend to newcomers—it was in the air, a sense that everyone there awaited and expected the presence of the others.

"Something felt so right," she wrote. "I left feeling happy."

But that wasn't the end of the welcome: the next day, she received an email from the pastor. "Dear Cheryl," it read; "Thanks so much for joining us for worship on Sunday. It was really great to meet you . . . and I hope you felt welcome and able to worship. . . . In any case, you . . . are very welcome, and next time you stop in, maybe we can talk a bit longer."

Cheryl admitted this could be great marketing on the church's part, but dismisses that interpretation. Maybe it was a hook, but "it's a hook I never had received. I could tell he cared about me." Young people are eager for a sense of welcome, of belonging— of *home*, in this case—and they know it when they find it. She returned the next week, and, unsurprisingly, "was greeted by more and more new friends, and felt lovingly welcomed into the arms of the congregation."

> 66 A culture of welcome can impact an entire organization, encouraging members to be the *welcomers* and not just the welcomed. 99

Whether seeking welcome in a church, a school, a workplace, or any other group, young people know the experience they want, even if they don't know how to describe just what it will look like when they arrive. Cultivating the value of welcoming is a powerful way to make sure a person knows that they are invited as a full participant, that they are safe, and that the organization has space for them. Giving someone this kind of experience is often a matter of simple, straightforward gestures of welcome: warm greetings, intentional connections, clear orientation, and so on. Despite the simplicity of these actions, they are powerful—and not just for young people. A culture of welcome can impact an entire organization, encouraging members to be the *welcomers* and not just the welcomed.

Bringing It All Together

Takeaways

1. To be welcomed is to be received warmly, greeted intentionally, and accepted without obstacle or condition upon arrival. Feeling welcomed, especially as a newcomer to a community or organization, means there is space prepared (emotionally, physically, spiritually, and so on).

2. Through a welcoming process of onboarding, a new employee can arrive with the unmistakable sense that their coworkers were expecting, even awaiting, their arrival. But perhaps even more important than small gestures or orienting materials is that a welcoming effort happens right on day one.

3. The role of safety in creating a sense of welcome is an important one, as it is nearly impossible for a person to feel welcomed if they don't feel safe. But more than that, if a person feels safe, they can participate more freely in the organization.

4. Making someone know they are invited as a full participant, they are safe, and there is space for them within the organization is often a matter of simple, straightforward gestures of welcome: warm greetings, intentional connections, clear orientation, and so on. Despite the simplicity of some of these actions, they are powerful—and not just for young people. A culture of welcome can impact an entire organization, encouraging members to be the *welcomers* and not just the welcomed.

✓ Act on the Data

☐ Imagine creating a "Welcoming Kit" for your organization. What would you include to help a new person understand your history or identity? How would that person's schedule help them get to know individuals and the whole group? Consider implementing a real welcome strategy, if you don't already have one, for both new members and those who may be on the periphery of joining—how might you welcome them in different ways?

☐ Safety makes it possible to feel welcome. What are things your community is already doing to cultivate a culture of safety for all members? Whether about individuals who identify as LGBTQ+, those with special needs, or young people in general, take something concrete—like your signage and website—and try to read it from an outsider's perspective. Does it tell a story of safety and welcome?

☐ Practicing and implementing the Belongingness Process in your relationships with young people can be as simple as learning and using a person's name. When you first learn a young person's name, confirm that you are using their expressed pronouns and proper pronunciation. Memorize their name and use it three times in conversation soon after learning it, and again at every passing or gathering.

Reflect on Your Experience

• A feeling of rich welcome can be hard to describe, but we offer some hallmarks here. What else would you add to the definition? What elements of welcome would appeal to you?

• Have you ever felt unwelcome in a space? What can you distill from that experience to aid you in becoming a more welcoming person or organization?

• Alternatively, what can you learn from an experience in which you truly felt welcomed?

REFERENCES

Doyle, Gabriel, et al. "Alignment at Work: Using Language to Distinguish the Internalization and Self-Regulation Components of Cultural Fit in Organizations." *Proceedings of the 55th Annual Meeting of the Association for Computational Linguistics* 1 (July 2017): 603–612.

"Family Creates Accessible Amusement Park for Daughter with Special Needs." ABC 30 Action News. December 19, 2019.

Fosslien, Liz, and Mollie West Duffy. "How to Foster a Culture of Belonging at Work." *Quartz at Work*, February 8, 2019.

"How Warby Parker Makes Every Point in Its Employee Lifecycle Extraordinary." *First Round Review,* March 1, 2018.

Morgan's Wonderland. The information about Morgan's Wonderland in this chapter is taken from the "About Us" section of the theme park's website with one exception: the quote from Gordon Hartman's interview with ABC 30 Action News.

Rozinkski, Cheryl. "Give Me Jesus." Blog. September 24, 2016.

Springtide Research Institute. *Belonging: Reconnecting America's Loneliest Generation.* Bloomington, MN: Springtide Research Institute, 2020. The sidebar "Welcome: The Beginning of Belonging" is excerpted with slight adaption from this report.

The Welcoming Project. The information about The Welcoming Project in this chapter is taken from the organization's website.

We Dine Together. The information about We Dine Together and Be Strong in this chapter is taken from the "About Us" section of the movement's website.

CHAPTER 5
IMPACTFUL

Avery was the quintessential first-year high school student: a combination of nervous and excited; ultimately eager to meet new friends—some of whom, she hoped, would share her enthusiasm for environmental justice. But while Avery herself spent time getting more involved in this particular interest, she was disappointed to find that her classmates didn't seem to care about this issue as much as she did.

"The culture at my high school was centered around sports," she remarked. "And if you weren't involved with sports or any after-school clubs, you didn't really belong there." Avery felt that her peers who got involved with academics or sports were connecting with one another more easily. Because Avery was focused on broader global issues like the environment instead of the typical events of high school life, she didn't feel she belonged.

Feeling left out was not the only disappointment though. She was discouraged to see an apparent lack of big-picture thinking about life outside and after high school—the kind she so deeply valued. "It was really hard feeling like I was the only one who cared about the state of my classmates and the planet. It made me question why I should even try if no one was willing to do the same. I wanted a place where discussions about something greater than myself were happening. I needed to be somewhere where people geeked out and bonded over recycling and nature."

Avery was seeking friendships and affiliations with people who shared her sense of social responsibility, a kind of kindred awareness of the bigger picture, outside the bubble of high school or the here and now of everyday life. She was seeking a culture that valued the importance of making a positive impact.

While Avery didn't find what she was looking for at this high school, her high regard for this value led her to keep looking until she found a space that would embody it for and with her. Before we get to that, though, this chapter explores the value of having a positive impact and what that can look like when embodied by different organizations.

IMPACT

Insights from Springtide Research

To be impactful is to practice social responsibility. But what is social responsibility? Social scientists define the value of *impactful* as having two fundamental commitments: actively engaging key social issues, and thoughtfully minimizing harm.

1. *Actively engaging key social issues.* Organizations take action in response to social issues through philanthropic and volunteer efforts, and they also adopt internal practices such as diversity, equity, and inclusion efforts.

This aspect of the value is often modeled *within* the culture of an organization. It can be a way of understanding that the responsibility for positive change in the world does not lie outside an organization but often starts within it. Hiring policies, volunteer mandates, workshops and continued education that raise awareness about social issues, and so on, are all ways leaders can foster an internal practice of social responsibility.

2. *Thoughtfully minimizing harmful consequences.* Organizations pay attention to their practices and seek to minimize any harm caused by them. This is especially clear in the case of environmental issues. For example, organizations can adopt sustainable practices and workflows for things like reducing or recycling waste, sourcing materials for products, designing buildings and landscapes, and making decisions about fuel sources.

This aspect of the value often looks outward and starts with the need for reflection: What are the consequences—both positive and negative—of the activities people do daily? How do individuals and organizations take responsibility for reducing any harmful consequences of that work, whether those are issues of environmental concern—as in the definition above—or issues of racial or gender discrimination, the diminishment and distribution of resources, especially for the poor, and so on?

In today's globalized markets and media, many young people are attuned to the interconnectedness of action and consequence on local, national, and global scales. They can turn on the news to see forest fires in California and simultaneously receive a text from a friend who has family in that area. Impact is immediate. Given this kind of social awareness, it's no surprise that young people overwhelmingly affirm the expectation that any organization that merits their affiliation should value making a positive impact.

In our research at Springtide, we found that many young people are right in line with Avery from the opening parts of this chapter. Our respondents place a high value on living impactful lives. They say they are attracted to organizations—schools, companies, civic organizations, religious communities—that pay attention to social issues and respond in meaningful ways to needs both within and beyond the organization. Our data suggest that they hold themselves to a high standard of being impactful as well.

For example, over half of our respondents agree that organizations (both for-profit and nonprofit) have a responsibility to contribute something good in the world. Significantly, these same respondents hold themselves to a similarly high level of accountability. Fifty-eight percent say that they feel it is important to do something good for society, and more than one in three report that *nothing* they do matters if it does not effect some good in the world.

More than one in three

young people surveyed report that **nothing they do matters** if it does not **promote some good in the world.**

SPRINGTIDE™ NATIONAL RESEARCH RESULTS
© 2020 Springtide. Cite, share, and join the conversation at springtideresearch.org.

In other words, young people are increasingly evaluating the work they do and the organizations they do it with through a broad lens. It's important to them to find leaders and organizations who share this same passion for doing good in the world, whether by actively engaging social issues head-on or thoughtfully minimizing harm.

66 Fifty-eight percent of young people surveyed say that they feel it is important to do something good for society. 99

Active Engagement with Key Social Issues

In the earlier example, Avery hoped that *in addition* to all the things one would expect to receive during high school (like the chance to encounter new ideas, try new activities, or make friends), she would also be able to engage wider social and environmental issues. She wanted her high school experience to do more than meet these basic expectations. She wanted it to provide opportunities for thinking beyond the walls of high school, academics, or sports.

> **❝** Practicing the value of social responsibility means actively engaging key social issues. For an organization, that means a willingness to talk about and do more than what's expected—it means a willingness to take responsibility for making a positive impact in ways that might be slightly outside its typical 'lane.' **❞**

Practicing the value of social responsibility means actively engaging key social issues. For an organization, that means a willingness to talk about and do more than what's expected—it means a willingness to take responsibility for making a positive impact in ways that might be slightly outside its typical "lane." A school's typical lane is education; a clothing company's usual lane is garments; for a church, synagogue, or mosque, that lane is often gathering a community of faith together for worship. But what if a church sought to be impactful outside its traditional lane?

Ascension Lutheran Church in South Burlington, Vermont, tries to live the value of being impactful. Though people may gather with one set of common values in mind—belief in particular creedal commitments and a desire for ritual, community, and connection to something bigger than themselves—Ascension does not stop there. Rev. Dr. Nancy Wright, the leader of the congregation, "sees herself as a pastor, a shepherd, and yet also as a seeker with other people for God's presence and love. She is especially interested in where God wants the church to bring healing in situations of poverty, injustice, and environmental degradation," according to one online biography.

Wright brings this environmental sensibility to her role as pastor of the congregation. Beginning in 2010, Ascension took on a project to clean up part of the local watershed, Bartlett Brook. The three-year project became the basis for a different kind of thinking about what churches are called to do, and Ascension developed a manual for other churches and organizations to begin their own "Watershed Discipleship."

The *Congregational Watershed Discipleship Manual*, coauthored by Wright and Richard Butz, describes the impact and import of this kind of commitment to do good in the world:

> **Caring for water orients a congregation in a new and deep way to its social, cultural, and ecological community, while also positioning it to develop supportive ties to other congregations and groups in the area to foster watershed health. When a congregation cares for its local watershed, it potentially promotes awareness and action to ameliorate worldwide water justice issues, including climate change and the feminization of poverty, both of which reflect and create water justice issues. (P. 7)**

And Ascension is having a wider impact: Wright is the environmental liaison for her regional denomination. The activities of her church have been spotlighted and praised by those invested in the earth's well-being and the church's thriving. By taking the demands of social responsibility seriously, Ascension Lutheran Church is expanding what *church* can mean and do.

Recall that more than 50% of the young people we surveyed agree that organizations have a responsibility to contribute some good to the world; nearly 60% hold themselves to the same standard of making a positive impact. Our research also shows that more than 70% say it is important that the organizations they are a part of intentionally work toward environmental sustainability. In addition, 55% agree it is important to them *personally* to look after the environment and care for nature to save life and resources.

More than
70%
of respondents say it is important that the organizations they are a part of **intentionally work toward environmental sustainability.**

More than
50%
of respondents agree that **organizations have a responsibility to contribute some good to the world.**

SPRINGTIDE™ NATIONAL RESEARCH RESULTS
© 2020 Springtide. Cite, share, and join the conversation at **springtideresearch.org.**

Organizations that commit to something greater than just what's expected—that insist on active engagement with key social issues—are organizations young people support. This may look like care for the earth from a faith community, or it may look like help providing childcare for single parents at a corporate work environment. It might look like workshops on race and gender identity with volunteers at a food bank, or it may look like efforts to create inclusive educational environments for those who are other-abled in physical and intellectual ways. Engaging key social issues head-on, in addition to whatever good work, service, or product you are already providing, is a crucial part of being impactful. And being impactful is an essential qualification for earning the respect of young people today.

ACT ⟩ ON THE DATA: Think about your typical or expected lane at your organization. Create a list of some of the most pressing or most local issues that face your community. Now compare the results of the brainstorming activity: How can you expand your lane to thoughtfully include one or two of the issues you named as concerns within your community? Involve others—both inside and outside your organization—to help expand your thinking and dialogue.

 ## B Corporations Attract Young People

The nonprofit organization B Lab certifies companies based on their commitment to *stakeholder* values, which is distinct from *shareholder* values, as it refers to those with stakes that aren't necessarily or exclusively financial: the environment and the employee, for example. Certified B Corporations "meet the highest standards of verified social and environmental performance, public transparency, and legal accountability to balance profit and purpose," according to the B Lab website.

Athleta, one of the largest certified clothing manufacturers, reports that since becoming certified in 2018, employee engagement, talent retention, and talent recruiting all spiked. In an article for the online blog site *Medium* ("Gen Z Is Shaping the Future of Work"), BBMG, a brand and innovation consultancy, quotes Athleta manager of strategic initiatives, Emily Allbritten: "We have so many candidates saying they want to interview with us because we are B Corp certified, because we have this purpose-driven brand." Young people are eager to affiliate with organizations that not only reflect their values for positive impact but also create opportunities to do good and reduce harm.

THOUGHTFULLY MINIMIZING HARM
Examples in the Clothing and Fashion Industry

In addition to engaging key social issues, impactful organizations thoughtfully reduce harmful consequences of their activity. This aspect of social responsibility often considers what's going on outside the organization's walls. What systems are at work in the world that this or that activity, this or that choice, directly affects? This kind of reflection leads impactful organizations to nuance or change their practices to reduce harm, whether, as in the examples below, those harms are affecting the earth, the employee, or the customer.

The Impact of Radical Transparency

A recent trend in the fashion industry is to reduce harmful impacts throughout the supply chain. This harm reduction sometimes concerns factory worker wages and conditions and other times environmental issues like water waste, plastic usage, and carbon footprints. There is even a push for transparency around cost and price discrepancy in an industry in which fast fashion and price gouging are both common practices.

Everlane is a clothing company launched in 2010 by Michael Preysman out of a commitment to *radical transparency*—a decision to lift the veil on the fashion industry.[1] He was concerned that a T-shirt might cost $6 to make but retail for $16 or $60 depending on the label attached to it. For Everlane, the founding principle of radical transparency has resulted in

---

[1] As we were going to press, Everlane came under scrutiny for "greenwashing"—making claims about sustainability and environmentalism that aren't entirely true—and for having an internal culture of racism. Regardless of what this scrutiny reveals, this book's observations about the brand's popularity being related to their public commitment to transparency remains largely true. Whether this brand will continue to be popular, for these or other reasons, is not yet clear.

numerous commitments, all of which amount to reducing harm: transparent pricing models to avoid the dual harms of fast fashion and price gouging, high ethical standards for the factories they work with (in terms of wages, conditions, and sustainability), and ambitious environmental practices for their clothes-making. These commitments show up in ways that are both internal and external.

While avoiding the pitfalls of fast fashion and price gouging, Everlane has created a cult-like customer base that includes a lot of young people. In large part, this is because Everlane reflects the values that young people want to practice themselves: to be an agent for good in the world. And that good impact extends not only to the environment but to workers and customers too. In an article for *Business Insider*, Gen Z consultant and researcher Jason Dorsey explains that young people "are very fiscally pragmatic and practical with their money. They are looking for value." This value can be through low prices or longer-lasting quality, he explains. Featured as an example later in the article, Everlane, with its commitment to radical transparency, intends to provide both.

For every product Everlane sells, they clearly offer the logic for its pricing and a detailed description—including pictures—about the factory in which it was made. On their website at the time of writing, a woman's gray turtleneck is listed for $35. Under the price, it notes "Traditional Retail: $75," a calculation based on the average industry markup of five to six times the cost of manufacturing. If you click the traditional retail price, it takes you to a section lower on the page that announces "Transparent Pricing: We believe customers have the right to know what their products cost to make." The materials, hardware, labor, duties, and transport combine to a true cost of $15.10 for this particular turtleneck.

Scrolling down to the details about this garment, customers learn that this piece was made at a factory in Lima, Peru. They can access a webpage dedicated to the factory, which discloses Everlane's relationship to the business, its standards and practices, and a bit about the owners. In this case, it reads, "A true family business, this small batch factory is operated by three self-made sisters who are motivated by transparency and ethical manufacturing methods," with pictures and detailed bios alongside.

Radical transparency is, in many ways, another way of expressing the value of being impactful—it is a way of denoting that a person or organization is aware of the way its activity in the world has consequences for others, and it is a commitment to recognizing and addressing those consequences head-on.

ACT **ON THE DATA:** What might a commitment to "radical transparency" look like if this principle were translated into the context of your organization? Ask young people who are involved in your group what questions they have about the systems, processes, and powers at work in your activities, and have candid conversations about some of those realities. What might you learn? What might they learn?

Back in Style: Reusing and Upcycling

The drive toward reducing harm within the fashion industry is not just corporation-led; it is a demand from buyers, an expectation at the behest of consumers—especially young consumers. And young people are not waiting for clothing brands to do all the work of reducing harm. They are taking up the cause themselves, communicating a strong message to organizations who aren't willing to act with regard to their social responsibilities.

Chief among these strong messages? The notable increased market for secondhand clothing. As a stance against fast fashion, a process for creating clothing that emphasizes the quick and cheap availability of trendy pieces to large markets, people have shown a renewed interest in reusing and upcycling secondhand clothing. Brick and mortar thrift and vintage stores have been around for some time, but online opportunities for secondhand sales are making this trend easily and widely accessible: thredUP, Etsy, The Break, The RealReal, and Poshmark, among many others, are rapidly growing e-commerce platforms for users to both sell and buy used clothing.

The US Chamber of Commerce comments on this trend in a September 2019 article by Joan Verdon: "Recommerce—the reselling of previously worn clothing—is secondhand shopping for the digital age." The article continues, noting the way recommerce meets the desired value of young people for reducing harm and creating good by addressing "the growing concern, especially on the part of younger consumers, that fast fashion and wear-once clothing is bad for the planet and that reselling clothes keeps them out of the landfills." ThredUp's annual Resale Report indicates that "millennials and Gen Z [are] adopting secondhand 2.5x faster than other age groups" and that "more than 1 in 3 Gen Z'ers will buy secondhand in 2019"— clear evidence that the importance of reducing harm, even while adding affordable pieces to one's wardrobe—is driving the fashion industry in a major way.

This commitment to environmental sustainability is unsurprising, given our findings that over 70% of the young people we surveyed indicated it is important that organizations they choose to participate in intentionally work toward sustainability through their decisions and actions. Being part of an organization doesn't just apply to the places young people chose to work or worship, but, of course, to where and what they consume.

Reducing harm in the fashion industry is trending—and young people are a huge part of the reason. As they commit themselves to doing good and reducing harm in the world, they expect the same of the places they spend their resources, whether time, money, or labor. Whether an organization sells garments or offers an education, whether it gathers people for worship or band practice or Little League, it is always possible—and important—to reduce harm. And the task of harm reduction always starts with reflection: What people or places are impacted by your group's activities? How can you take small steps to alleviate any negative consequences of those activities—carpooling? composting? recycling or upcycling? something else?

ACT ON THE DATA: Social responsibility takes many forms. But one sure way to capture the imaginations of young people is to demonstrate environmental awareness and care. Create opportunities in your organization for young people to engage in environmental activism and learning, possibly through participation in local activism opportunities, or inviting guest speakers on related topics.

BUILDING CULTURALLY RESPONSIBLE CULTURES

Eager to be connected with peers and mentors who cared about the environment and practiced intentional social responsibility, Avery transferred to a high school with an environmentally focused curriculum. Now a senior, she said she had found her impactful community. "As juniors, we learned about the fundamental aspects of community. And we did a lot of group work. Once those friendships were formed, we focused on being environmentally friendly at school and also out in the world."

Active participation in large- and small-scale environmental justice efforts is the norm at Avery's school. She and her classmates participated in the September 2019 student walkout for climate justice. The administration supported it, and the students enthusiastically participated. As one teacher explained, "These activities foster community, communication, and good old-fashioned teamwork."

One of Avery's first projects involved studying the health of a local pond. She and her group mates measured the amount of agricultural runoff and the diversity of the flora in the pond, eventually providing the data they collected to the state's Department of Natural Resources. Another student-led project changed the trash can labels in the lunchroom to "landfill," with the hope of encouraging people to compost and recycle. As someone not only interested in, but deeply committed to, the health of the earth, Avery is among peers.

And this sense of kinship matters: sharing a core belief can alleviate some of the relational stress young people often feel in high school. "It's nice knowing that you're on the same page when it comes to the environment. We'll be in study hall and start talking about climate change, plan to attend a protest, or pull out our phones and watch the news. They aren't superficial conversations."

Avery's new school has given her a place to make impactful choices alongside like-minded peers. "I have my community," says Avery. "And I have somewhere I belong."

This sense of community and belonging is directly related to the way Avery's new school practices the value of being impactful. Her high school doesn't settle on simply providing an education rooted in traditional curriculum. Instead it strives to actively engage social issues—encouraging climate activism among its students—and to reduce harm, as in their commitment to composting what might otherwise end up in the trash. These examples, specific to a sense of social responsibility tied directly to the environment (though social responsibility concerns itself with myriad other social issues), are integral to being impactful and integral to Avery's enthusiasm to be a part of this institution.

Bringing It All Together

Takeaways

1. To be impactful is to practice social responsibility. Social scientists define the value of *impactful* as having two fundamental commitments: actively engaging key social issues, and thoughtfully minimizing harm.

2. Over half of Springtide's respondents indicated that organizations (both for-profit and nonprofit) have a responsibility to contribute something good in the world. Significantly, these same respondents held themselves to a similarly high level of accountability. Fifty-eight percent told us that they feel it is important to do something good for society, and one in three reported that *nothing* they do matters if it does not do some good in the world.

3. Practicing the value of social responsibility means actively engaging key social issues. For an organization, that means a willingness to talk about and do more than what's expected; it means a willingness to take responsibility for making a positive impact in ways that might be slightly outside their typical lane.

4. Impactful organizations thoughtfully reduce harmful consequences of their activity. This aspect of social responsibility often considers what's going on *outside* the organization's walls. What systems are at work in the world that this or that activity, this or that choice, directly affects? This kind of reflection leads impactful organizations to nuance or change their practices to reduce harm—whether . . . those harms are affecting the earth, the employee, or the customer.

√ Act on the Data

❑ Think about what your typical or expected lane is at your organization. Create a list of some of the most pressing or most local issues that face your community. Now compare the brainstorming activity: How can you expand your lane to thoughtfully include one or two of the issues you named as concerns within your community? Involve others—both inside and outside your organization—to help expand your thinking and dialogue.

❑ What might a commitment to "radical transparency" look like if this principle were translated into the context of your organization? Ask young people who are involved in your group what questions they have about the systems and processes and powers at work in your activities, and have candid conversations about some of those realities. What might you learn? What might they learn?

❑ Social responsibility takes many forms. But one sure way to capture the imaginations of young people is to demonstrate environmental awareness and care. Create opportunities in your organization for young people to engage in environmental activism and learning, possibly through participation in local activism opportunities, or by inviting guest speakers on related topics.

Reflect on Your Experience

• Imagine a B Corp-type certification process for religious and other nonprofit organizations, which would consider the value of the organization for the environment, the local community, and employees. Would any organization you are a part of need to make changes to qualify? If so, what is the likelihood that such changes would attract more young people to your organization?

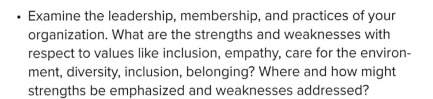

- Examine the leadership, membership, and practices of your organization. What are the strengths and weaknesses with respect to values like inclusion, empathy, care for the environment, diversity, inclusion, belonging? Where and how might strengths be emphasized and weaknesses addressed?

REFERENCES

BBMG. "Gen Z Is Shaping the Future of Work." *Medium*, December 3, 2019.

Butz, Richard, and Nancy Wright. *Congregational Watershed Discipleship Manual: Faith Communities as Stewards of the World's Waters*. East Dummerston, VT: Lone Leaf Publishing, 2018.

Hanbury, Mary. "Gen Z Is Leading an Evolution in Shopping That Could Kill Brands as We Know Them." *Business Insider*, 2019.

Our Children, Climate Faith Conference website is the source of biographical information about Nancy Wright.

Reinhart, James et al. "ThredUP Annual Resale Report." 2019.

Verdon, Joan. "The Rise of the Resale Market." US Chamber of Commerce. September 16, 2019.

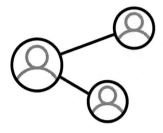

CHAPTER 6

RELATIONAL

Serena was the kind of person who was eager for deep, tight-knit relationships. Whether in her home life, volunteering, interning, or at college, she hoped to form deeper connections: the kind of friendships a person depends on during life's more challenging or emotionally charged moments, the kind a person turns to when sharing moments of deep questioning and also great joy.

However, Serena noted that many contexts didn't seem conducive to deep exchanges. "Frat parties, other more conventional college gatherings lacked meaning and purpose and deep connection. They were more on a surface level," she remarked. Dissatisfied, she was confused about why others seemed so content with more surface-level relationships. "I was asking myself, 'What's wrong with me, why am I unable to make friends?'"

Serena's desire for deep friendships may be particular to her context, but it's not unique: it is a universal hope to have close, trusting connections. And it is often in the throes of early adulthood that these kinds of relationships are first forged.

What Serena may already have—indeed, what might be found at the parties or conventional gatherings where she *wasn't* finding more substantive relationships—were acquaintances. These types of relationships are valuable as well, as they form a web of connections, even if the bonds amid those connections are shallower.

While Serena didn't find these closer relationships during her first year at college, she had more success that summer. Serena spent her time on a communal farm near her hometown doing yoga teacher training, among other things. "It was a small community of people, about 15 of us, all ages," from senior adults to Serena, the youngest. "Everyone told stories of their lives, shared what they were going through. We're all going through things every step of our lives." Serena was glimpsing what closer bonds might look and feel like—and, importantly, where and how to find them.

For instance, these weren't the kinds of conversations that could happen casually at parties, but rather developed after much time, energy, and space has been spent together. The relationships she cultivated with this summertime community were a taste of meaningful and life-giving connections, even prompting greater empathy in Serena and the others: "If we could carry the understanding that we all go through stuff, we are all human, we would be nicer to each other. When we find belonging and purpose in our lives, then we tackle the bigger things."

The time she spent on the farm planted a seed of hope in Serena: maybe she could cultivate this sort of community on campus. It would take courage and creativity. But on the farm, she had experienced the intimacy she craved. It could happen.

Serena carried that hope with her into her second year of college. She found she wasn't alone. The chapter returns to Serena's experience after exploring what Springtide Research, as well as other sources, have to say about the importance young people attach to this relational quality in their lives.

RELATIONAL CONNECTION
Insights from Springtide Research

Serena wanted more than mere surface relationships at college. She hoped to form deeper bonds with people than typical campus activities naturally afforded. This desire for substantial relationships is a powerful and important one that most humans share. Social scientists call these deep, authentic, and life-giving relationships *bonding relationships.*

Bonding relationships are defined by reciprocity: mutual sharing, kindness that begets more kindness, and a give-and-take in nearly all aspects of the connection. Bonding relationships are those foundational relationships that a person can rely on: close friends, family, or other relationships of love and trust. They can confer a sense of safety, identity, purpose, and place in the world.

The kinds of relationships Serena might have made in the classroom or at a party—more casual relationships with less vulnerability and depth, but still important to maintain—are what social scientists call *bridging relationships.* This term applies to something closer to acquaintances, as bridging relationships describe a more extended network of relations. While bonding relationships make a person feel safe and cared for, bridging relationships widen the circle, expanding a person and their network through new ideas, new opportunities, and new people.

BONDING RELATIONSHIPS
are deep, authentic, and life-giving relationships.

BRIDGING RELATIONSHIPS
broaden a person's network through more casual connections.

> **66** While bonding relationships make a person feel safe and cared for, bridging relationships widen the circle, expanding a person and their network through new ideas, new opportunities, and new people. **99**

To not only survive but thrive, young people need both bridging and bonding relationships in their lives. Too many bridging relationships and, as in Serena's case, connections can start to feel shallow instead of just casual. Too many bonding relationships overwhelm in the other way since, given the importance of reciprocity and mutuality, a person can only sustain so many of these deep relationships at a time.

Relational connection emerges in Springtide data as a key driver for young people when making choices about belonging to organizations, committing to workplaces, and choosing where to spend their time in general. Our findings confirmed the value of both bonding and bridging relationships as important, even critical, to the young people we surveyed.

When we asked specifically about the workplace—either current or future—we clearly saw the value of both bridging and bonding relationships. Nearly 50% of those surveyed say they value or would value having workplace colleagues as friends; in other words, they want bonding relationships at work. And 43% agree that leaders in a workplace should encourage opportunities for social engagement among employees and even provide the means to foster these. They want bonds and bridges in the relationships at their workplaces.

The high value placed on relationships by young people is a fundamental determinant of their commitment and loyalty. Nearly one in three (32%) young people say they will stay involved with an organization *only* if they have friends there, and 38% say organizations they are a part of need to offer time for socializing with others in the organization. This is a strong indication that young people are eager for occasions to form bridging relationships as well.

43%
of respondents agree leaders in a workplace should **encourage opportunities for social engagement among employees.**

Nearly 50%
of respondents say that they value or would **value having workplace colleagues as friends.**

SPRINGTIDE™ NATIONAL RESEARCH RESULTS
© 2020 Springtide. Cite, share, and join the conversation at springtideresearch.org.

Additionally, relationships are at the heart of how young people make meaning in their organizations. Nearly 60% of the young people we surveyed indicate it is important that organizations they choose to participate in value and foster deep relationships that center on service to others, highlighting the desire for both bonding and bridging relationships to be built into the culture of the organizations they work in and with.

Social observers, health-care providers and advocates, researchers, and others have reported extensively on the rising effect of loneliness in this country. Young people more than people of other age-groups suffer loneliness, manifested clinically in rising rates of anxiety, depression, and even suicide. Leaders who work with young people can make a difference by organizing, sponsoring, and facilitating organizations and workplaces that encourage well-being and build meaningful relationships in their lives.

Organizations that attract young people encourage and enable both bonding and bridging relationships to thrive create a truly relational experience. Such organizations exist in a variety of settings and contexts—professional, social, and cultural. But they can seem difficult to locate in an increasingly virtual society, and they can feel risky to try. The rewards, however, justify the effort.

At a time of pervasive loneliness in this country, especially among young people, we hear from them a strong desire for human connection—for relationships. The discussion that follows explores that desire—as it is experienced at college, in the workplace, and in the larger community. It also provides examples of how leaders can effectively bring relationship-building into the organizations they lead and the young lives of those they serve.

BRIDGING AND BONDING CONNECTIONS

Springtide data confirm that young people desire bridging relationships—the kind of connections and networks that are casual but still extremely meaningful. Walking into a classroom or office and recognizing friendly faces, feeling a sense of belonging on a sports team or board meeting: these kinds of connections are important. The people in that classroom, office, team, or meeting may not be best friends with one another, but they share relationships of great worth.

Sometimes these bridging relationships can be difficult to build and maintain. But the ability and opportunity to do so is valuable because it is often from the wide network of bridging relation-ships that bonding relationships are first found.

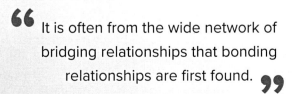

66 It is often from the wide network of bridging relationships that bonding relationships are first found. **99**

Dr. Varun Soni, dean of religious life at the University of Southern California (USC), writes in a July 2019 op-ed for the *Los Angeles Times*:

> **What I have noticed in my work with students is that many of them face the same hidden root challenge: loneliness. . . . I never got the question in my first five years at USC that I now get almost daily from students: "How do I make friends?" Students may have thousands of friends online, but few in real life; they may be experts at talking with their thumbs, but not so much with their tongues. As a result, many feel as though they don't have a tribe or a sense of belonging. They feel disconnected from what it means to be human.**

USC has taken positive steps to address this issue of on-campus loneliness. These include a dedicated mindfulness training app and free mindfulness programs; a for-credit first-year course that focuses on emotional intelligence, healthy relationships, self-care, resiliency, and human flourishing; a new artificial intelligence well-being assistant; classes on making meaningful relationships at USC; yoga classes, drum circles, friendship courses, community teas, laughing groups, and connection workshops.

Recently the campus appointed its first director of belonging. Among other responsibilities, she teaches classes on making meaningful relationships at USC through its Campfires program. Campfires are conversations that USC describes as groups of two or three or larger where participants begin by surrendering laptops and phones to the center of the gathering and then watching a video, followed by a period of asking one another questions.

The questions are intended "to move people from acquaintance into deeper connection with each other," according to the Office of Religious and Spiritual Life website. Clear guidelines for asking and responding to questions are provided, and student leaders are trained in the "'arts of Campfires' in order to make their campus organizations more conducive to the formation of meaningful relationships among their members."

To be clear, meaningful connections don't have to be vulnerable or intimate. It's meaningful to connect with someone over a shared love for a local baseball team or a favorite food. Those shared preferences might form the foundation for working together on an upcoming project, which may lead to more bonding. Or it may not. The point isn't collecting bonding relationships but forming meaningful connections at a variety of depth levels.

Initiating and developing both bridging and bonding relation-ships is sometimes challenging for young people today. Their social skills or experiences have been formed with different priorities than other generations—and that's okay. But it means that institutions like schools, houses of worship, and workplaces now carry the onus of creating spaces and structures to facilitate bridging and bonding for and among young people.

ACT ON THE DATA: Bridging relationships are often the seed for bonding relationships. Young people need both. Don't underestimate the value of the bridging opportunities—chances for a wide net of people to gather—you provide in your caring for young people.

FOSTERING FRIENDSHIPS AT WORK

When asked about the workplace—either current or future— nearly half of young people surveyed by Springtide said that they value or would value having friends as workplace colleagues. Further, 43% say leaders should encourage oppor-tunities for social engagement among employees and even provide the means to do so.

Other data support these findings. In the 2018 article "The Work Connectivity Study," Future Workplace, a human resources advisory and research firm, reported the results of survey data gathered from more than 2,000 managers and employees from ten countries. The study, "Global Work Connectivity," found that one's longevity at a company correlates with having friends in the workplace.

Sixty percent of respondents reported that if they had more friends at work, they'd be inclined to stay with their current employers longer. When looking at generations separately, the researchers found that having friends is a stronger factor for workplace longevity for younger workers (74% of Gen Z and 69% of Millennial respondents) than for older workers (59% of Gen X and 40% of Baby Boomer respondents).

The survey respondents further suggest that workplace leaders can increase workers' longevity at the job by encouraging in-person connections between workers. Forty-five percent of respondents recommended team-building activities and social events while 31% recommended "workations"—travel away from home and office that blends leisure and work.[1]

"As much as people stereotype [young people] as always having their heads in their phones, Gen Z is also the generation that's craving the most personal contact" at work, says Anna Blue, co-executive director of Girl Up, as reported in a 2019 *Forbes* article by Manon DeFelice. "They want in-person relationships with their managers; they want to see their colleagues and have face-to-face collaboration because they've been missing so much of that being on their phones."

Chapter 3 of this book, on the value of authenticity, unpacks this phenomenon even more. Contrary to the stereotype, young

---

[1] The full findings are available in Dan Schawbel's 2018 book *Back to Human: How Great Leaders Create Connection in the Age of Isolation,* published by Da Capo Lifelong Books.

people often use technology in a thoughtful way. Still, a thoughtful virtual community only echoes what is desired and hoped for within in-person relationships: connection, honesty, creativity, and reciprocity. Like the value of relationality, the value of authenticity is reciprocal: the more authentically a person or organization acts, the more they invite others to do the same.

> 66 As much as people stereotype [young people]
> as always having their heads in their phones,
> Gen Z is also the generation that's craving
> the most personal contact. 99

"There's a social aspect about going to work that they don't want taken away," says Blue.

Work is the place many people spend the majority of their time. It's no surprise that young people want to spend that time meaningfully connecting with those with whom they work. And although the value of bridging and bonding may be especially clear in the workplace illustration, the logic applies to many contexts. **Wherever a young person experiences a real sense of relationship—whether bridging or bonding—they are more likely to feel they belong. This sense of belonging becomes the backdrop of safety needed to explore, create, and connect in even broader ways.**

ACT > ON THE DATA: The importance of bonding relationships cannot be overstated. But they can be hard to facilitate. Consider the example from Serena, who spent an entire summer sharing a space, meals, experiences, and conversations with her group. Try to imagine what your organization can do to help facilitate deeper bonds among members, and experiment with implementing different possibilities.

The Springtide report on isolation among young people, *Belonging: Reconnecting America's Loneliest Generation*, makes the importance of bridging and bonding relationships strikingly clear. The presence of even *one* trusted adult relationship—and trust can exist in bridges or bonds—reduces the experience of severe isolation in young people by half.

 ## Resilience and Belonging: Insights from Two Studies on the Importance of Being Relational

In a 2019 article, researchers Tracy Evans-Whipp and Constantine Gasser report on the study "Growing Up in Australia: The Longitudinal Study of Australian Children," which has followed the lives of around 10,000 children since 2004. When the older children in the study were 16–17 years old, they were asked about aspects of their lives, including their relationships with peers, their response to stressful life events such as loss or failure, and their ability to adapt to change.

"One aspect of teen well-being we looked at was resilience," the researchers report. "This is the ability to bounce back from stressful life events and learn and grow from them." The study discovered a close link between having at least one good friend and having more resilience to face some of life's hardships.

"[A] key finding from our research is that one of the best things you can do to foster resilience in a young person is to help them find and make friends. One good friend can make a big difference," conclude Evans-Whipp and Gasser.

Springtide's inaugural research report, *Belonging: Reconnecting America's Loneliest Generation,* also emphasizes the importance of relationships, in particular, with trusted adults in the lives of young people.

Young people today are reporting some of the highest rates of loneliness and isolation on record, with 33% saying they feel completely alone much of the time, and nearly 40% telling us they have no one in their lives to talk to. But there's hope: Springtide data also show that the presence of just one trusted adult in a young person's life cuts severe isolation in half.

ACT **ON THE DATA:** Research from two studies outside the purview of this book confirms the importance of relationships for the flourishing of young people. Each study emphasizes a different kind of relationship: with peers and with trusted adults. Which of these two kinds of relationships can your organization naturally foster? Think about new ways you might strengthen the opportunities for creating these kinds of bonds within your group.

SOCIAL COURAGE AND MEANINGFUL CONNECTIONS

After that lonely first year, Serena returned to school "inspired to try and build communities and experiences of change, to help people realize the only reason we're not friends is we lack the context to know each other." She began inviting peers into her home for weekly gatherings and conversations, hoping to create meaningful connections among people who would otherwise be strangers.

"I wanted to create physical space where we might step outside of our fast-paced and busy life where we make judgments and label each other," she said. "It's humbling to experience the multidimensionality of people. In these gatherings, we were opening up about siblings, passions, worries."

Over the next few years, Serena estimates she had created as many as fifty such gatherings. "All it takes is social courage for people to build spaces and open up," she said.

Serena now lives in San Francisco, where she works as community manager for a venture capital firm. "As community manager, I spend my days working to create meaningful human connections at every community event we host, each online interaction we enable, and every mentorship relationship we make happen."

Like many young people, Serena says she doesn't participate in organized religion, but after an overall positive religious upbringing, says she is "still figuring out what my religion and community in this modern world look like." And she's taking a cue from her college years: "I'm trying neighborhood potlucks, inviting people over for dinner. It's super awkward at first, but people show up. People are craving community. We are not lacking community in terms of gathering in space or digitally; but how can we create more meaningful gatherings, communities, connections?" Serena remarked. "People really are craving that. I used to look at these issues of community, belonging, loneliness, almost like downplaying the importance of it, that there are more pressing or urgent issues to focus on, such as climate change or homelessness.

"These questions of belonging and purpose are important on a different plane, however. When people feel connected, empathetic, that stuff is very powerful. In society now we feel disconnected." Citing change theory, Serena says, "when we get to know people intimately, as neighbors, not as strangers, then we can have greater empathy for the other, those not similar to us. Meaningful community and meaningful connection are the ways to get there."

Serena had arrived on campus looking for human connection on a meaningful level. When she didn't find the relational opportunities she sought, she created them. Adult leaders are in a position to respond to this desire for bridging and bonding relationships that so many young people tell us they value. It's not only good for young people—combating loneliness and creating meaningful relationships—it's good for organizations. Young people are like all people: hoping to find their place in the world and experience the security that comes from true belonging. When people find spaces that are truly relational, they don't give them up easily.

Bringing It All Together

Takeaways

1. While bonding relationships make a person feel safe and cared for, bridging relationships widen the circle, expanding a person and their network through new ideas, new opportunities, and new people.

2. At a time of pervasive loneliness in this country, especially among young people, we hear from them a strong desire for human connection—for relationships.

3. Sometimes these bridging relationships can be difficult to build and maintain. But the ability and opportunity to do so is important because it is often from the wide network of bridging relationships that bonding relationships are first found.

4. Wherever a young person experiences a real sense of relationship—whether bridging or bonding—they are more likely to feel they belong. This sense of belonging becomes the backdrop of safety needed to explore, create, and connect in even broader ways.

✓ Act on the Data

❑ Bridging relationships are often the seed for bonding relationships. Young people need both. Don't underestimate the value of the bridging opportunities—chances for a wide net of people to gather—you provide in your caring for young people.

❑ The importance of bonding relationships cannot be overstated. But they can be hard to facilitate. Consider the example from Serena, who spent an entire summer sharing a space, meals, experiences, and conversations with her group. Try to imagine what your organization can do to help facilitate deeper bonds among members, and experiment with implementing different possibilities.

❑ Research from two studies outside the purview of this book confirms the importance of relationships for the flourishing of young people. Each study emphasizes a different kind of relationship: with peers and with trusted adults. Which of these two kinds of relationships can your organization naturally foster? Think about new ways you might strengthen the opportunities for creating these kinds of bonds within your group.

Reflect on Your Experience

• Identify an organization in your community that young people freely choose to affiliate with. To what extent does the opportunity to develop friendships fuel the young people's participation? To find out, ask several of these young people.

• Are you familiar with thriving intergenerational communities that incorporate young people ages 13 to 25 in meaningful ways? If yes, how does the opportunity to develop bridging or bonding relationships affect their participation? How do these intergenerational communities foster these relationships?

- Have you witnessed a socially courageous initiative that increased genuine belonging and friendship-building among young people? If yes, can you identify the keys to the initiative's effectiveness?

REFERENCES

DeFelice, Manon. "What Gen Z Wants at Work Will Blow Your Mind," October 31, 2019. Available on the *Forbes* website.

Evans-Whipp, Tracy, and Constantine Gasser. "Teens with at Least One Close Friend Can Better Cope with Stress Than Those Without." *The Conversation,* November 24, 2019.

Soni, Varun. "There's a Loneliness Crisis on College Campuses." *Los Angeles Times,* July 14, 2019.

Springtide Research Institute. *Belonging: Reconnecting America's Loneliest Generation.* Bloomington, MN: Springtide Research Institute, 2020.

University of Southern California (USC). Information about USC's initiatives including Campfires was taken from the website of the university's Office of Religious and Spiritual Life.

CHAPTER 7

GROWTHFUL

"Everyone experiences growth in their own ways, whatever they're going through amid life's ups and downs," said James, a nursing student and a talented musician.

Not everyone sees the *downs* as growth, but for some people, like James, even setbacks, restarts, or flat no's have a way of becoming opportunities and occasions for creatively opening new doors or seeking new paths. Flexible, adaptable, and driven by a strong sense of what he wants, James isn't easily discouraged.

His interest in music began when he was young. After a few years of playing an instrument, James took up another one. He didn't *give up* the first instrument but just took up a second. "I think it was the first time in my life I took hold of something and made it my own," he recalled. Relentlessly curious and dedicated to constant learning, he eventually learned cello, piano, clarinet, and tuba. He played all before high school, and all with considerable skill.

"I discovered my passions—for music and other interests— simply by exploring, by being curious about the world and developing my perspective."

When his curiosity and sense of exploration led him to try per-cussion, his band teacher said no—he was already excelling at his current instrument. Not one to be discouraged, James found a way to make it work. Despite lacking any formal training in percussion, he auditioned for the percussion section of a tri-city honors youth orchestra, and he was admitted. The condition of acceptance to the honors orchestra was that he *also* be admitted to his school's percussion section—which he promptly was. Driven to keep learning and growing, he found a creative work-around and mastered yet another instrument.

Though skilled on and interested in many instruments, James ultimately decided to focus his attention on the flute. A high school classmate was also a flutist, and, James said, she "was brilliant. She was, like, a star." James could have felt discouraged by the talent of his peer, especially after deciding to focus on one instrument. Instead, he took this opportunity to grow.

In many ways, James embodies what it means to practice the value of being growthful. He has a disposition of constant curiosity and self-improvement. He is creative in the face of obstacles and encouraged by difficulties rather than put off by them. And despite being overshadowed by a more talented peer, James didn't feel discouraged. But before getting to more of his story, this chapter unpacks the meaning of being growthful and explores some ways this value shows up in organizations.

GROWTH
Insights from Springtide Research

Valuing growth may seem straightforward on the surface: a commitment to learning, exploring, and improving. But growing isn't just about forward motion or skill-building. It's deeper than that: a kind of disposition in the face of adversity. It's a value that young people embrace and embody as a way of understanding that the world around them is constantly changing, and so remaining static is a liability. Keeping doors open and responding creatively to setbacks is about survival and flexibility. In fact, at its core, growth is about adaptability and flexibility. As a value that drives people, it is rooted in a sense that one is never quite done "becoming" who they are.

Younger generations understand learning not as something confined to educational settings or a particular time of life. Instead, they understand that the job they want today may not exist in the future, and they are prepared to be lifelong learners and growers. In this sense, striving to grow is both a value of self-improvement and a safety net against the unknowns that inevitably come in life.

This understanding drives them to organizations where they can gain new knowledge, skills, and experiences—not just credentials and degrees. Whether in their career or volunteer activities, they want opportunities and resources to support growth and learning.

A commitment to personal learning and adaptability in the face of adversity is not unique to James's story. Springtide findings indicate the high regard many young people have for this value. Our survey data show that more than one out of three young people say that it's very important to them to make a conscious and dedicated effort to develop their own body, mind, and spirit. Two activities that 40% of young people say are very important to allow time and space for—activating the imagination and engaging in play—help people develop these aspects of themselves.

Not only do young people embrace these values for themselves, but they also expect the organizations they join to facilitate growth. Forty-five percent agree that they would consider working for less pay if the workplace supported their growth, learning, and professional development. And 46% agree that it is not worth their time to engage in an organization if it does not offer opportunities to grow and learn.

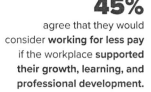

45%

agree that they would consider **working for less pay** if the workplace **supported their growth, learning, and professional development.**

46%

agree that it is **not worth their time** to engage in an **organization if it does not offer opportunities** to grow and learn.

SPRINGTIDE™ NATIONAL RESEARCH RESULTS
© 2020 Springtide. Cite, share, and join the conversation at springtideresearch.org.

Like James, 52% agree that after failure or a difficult situation, they always look for lessons that will help them to grow as a person. Instead of being discouraged by setbacks or failures, young people take these as facts of life, and continue adapting, growing, and seeking opportunities to respond creatively to difficulties. Young people want the chance to grow at work and in life in general, at times recognizing its long-term value even over the immediate promise of a big paycheck or guaranteed success.

This chapter explores organizations that embody and facilitate the value of growth in innovative and exemplary ways. The goal is not to hold these organizations up as the *only* ways to support growth and learning but to bring this multifaceted definition to life with real-life examples.

SELF-IMPROVEMENT AND SAFETY NETS

One of the simplest aspects of growing is through learning and being stretched outside a person's comfort zone. This aspect of growth is rooted in a desire to keep expanding and becoming, both for the sake of self-improvement and also to avoid falling behind in a rapidly changing world.

Young people want to continually expand their sense of self and their sets of skills. With more than one-third of young people telling us they think it's very important to develop their minds, bodies, and spirits, it's increasingly necessary that organizations find ways to provide such opportunities. The Awake Youth Project, a mindfulness and meditation program that partners with local high schools in Brooklyn, New York, does just that.

The mission statement on their website reads: "Inspired by the practice of mindfulness and its unwavering ability to awaken the mind towards liberation, peace and healing, Awake Youth Project (AYP) was created to offer a resting place, a space of transformation for Brooklyn's teens. Through our programming youth receive tools that aim to bolster their full potential in becoming more aware and deeply connected to their authentic selves." Authenticity, self-awareness, and growth toward total fullness: all critical aspects of practicing the value of being growthful.

AYP provides after-school drop-in meditation time, internships, professional development, and retreats. They also provide peer leadership training, which "teaches, supports and mentors a small, motivated group of teens and young adults (ages 15–21) in a 5-month intensive practice and exploration of mindfulness and meditation tools for everyday living, health and well-being." Testimonials on the AYP website make it clear that this kind of self-work has repercussions for young people's whole selves and whole lives.

"Learning how to understand how my emotions take place within my body has given me the chance to be with my mind and body in better harmony," wrote Armani, a young woman involved in the program. A young man, Richardson, said, "Before I started meditating, I would be overcome with anger and frustration quickly. Now, I have the chance to make a choice about how I react to my life and environment."

The skills these young people are acquiring are not just about self-improvement but are instances of a broader social outreach to an underserved, under-acknowledged community in the Bronx. The project's website cites studies that show the value of mindfulness intervention and notes that these "interventions reduce feelings of distress, anxiety and depression in addition to addressing other public health challenges facing our youth in under-acknowledged neighborhoods." AYP is the kind of program that demonstrates the way being growthful is a value of self-improvement both for its own sake *and* for the sake of preparing young people to face and overcome life's inevitable obstacles.

This principle is illumined by AYP, but it can be embodied by all types of organizations. Any group that hopes to have young people as members can and should adopt practices that facilitate growth. Synagogues, schools, companies, and communities of all types have skill-building opportunities and perspectives to offer young people that can impact their whole lives, even outside the formal boundaries of those institutional walls or set gatherings.

> **❝** Any group that hopes to have young people as members can and should adopt practices that facilitate growth. Synagogues, schools, companies, and communities of all types have skill-building opportunities and perspectives to offer young people that can impact their whole lives, even outside the formal boundaries of those institutional walls or set gatherings. **❞**

ACT > ON THE DATA: Think about the "life skills" your organization can help young people develop, even if it's not formally part of what you do. How can you offer these skills or perspectives to young people in a way that both encourages self-improvement and helps prepare them for the ups and downs of the real world?

FAST-PACED AND FLEXIBLE IN THE WORKPLACE

Young people are going to bring the desire to grow to any new place they enter or world they occupy, whether school, home life, digital relationships, or the workforce. With 45% of young people Springtide surveyed agreeing that they would consider working for less pay if the workplace supported their growth, learning, and professional development, there's an expectation that a work environment will not just support growth but also help facilitate this value in the life of a young person.

An article from *Accounting Today* highlights this value as it pertains to the youngest generation entering the workforce. Discussing a survey conducted by his firm, Larry Nash, US recruiting leader for Ernst & Young, says their "findings re-affirm what we already knew—this generation is driven, passionate and open-minded. They also place a strong emphasis on flexibility and opportunities for growth."

Open-minded, flexible, and eager for opportunities for growth—these are three qualities that describe young people, and three qualities that can describe an organization that matches and mirrors the high value they place on growing and learning.

> **66** Open-minded, flexible, and eager for opportunities for growth—these are three qualities that describe young people, and three qualities that can describe an organization that matches and mirrors the high value they place on growing and learning. **99**

"[Like young people], we are optimistic about the future, as we continue to evolve alongside them and adapt to disruption and the changing global workplace," Nash continues. Rather than clinging tightly to what *is*, organizations may consider relaxing their grip on certain routines, systems, and symbols. Take a cue from young people: 52% agree that after a failure or difficult situation, there are lessons to be sought. By keeping an open mind, communities of all types can slowly shift their culture to be flexible in the face of change and disruption. They can learn not only to expect the unexpected but to respond creatively to unforeseen shifts.

Emily Poague, vice president of marketing for LinkedIn Learning, discusses this same hallmark of growth for the newest generation entering the workforce. From their surveys of young people, which specifically aimed to assess trends in learning, they found that "nearly all agree skills today are changing faster than ever," with 76% of those surveyed confirming "that the skills necessary in today's workforce are different from the skills necessary in past generations." Fifty-nine percent of young people in this survey don't expect their job to exist in its current iteration in 20 years. **Springtide data suggest that organizations shouldn't be discouraged, but excited. Young people are adaptable, flexible, and growth-oriented. They'll commit to learning now what they might need for the future.**

Every club or company has the choice about whether to be intimidated by the possibility of paradigm shifts and unknowns in the future, or to prepare for the known possibility. Taking a cue from young people can help an organization adopt a more growthful disposition—one that can help it stay afloat, adapting as new realities shift and change in a fast-paced world.

ACT > ON THE DATA: Young people want to be a part of a culture that is growthful. The easiest way to implement and embody this value is by offering opportunities for learning and skill-building through your organization. What can or should a young person learn or gain by spending time with you or your group? How can you make this kind of learning more formal or official within your organization?

"POP-UP, POP-OUT, PUSH-THROUGH"

Growthful is an apt value for describing the first months of the year 2020. COVID-19 has underscored the importance of this value in the life of young people and the organizations that hope to serve them. The global pandemic forced many communities, companies, and groups to rethink how to work, gather, adapt, and survive.

The organizations that translated their mission through new technologies and extended their reach in innovative ways did so with a growthful disposition: by being adaptable, flexible, curious, and hopeful in the face of obstacles.

In an April 2020 article titled "Radically Adapting to the New World" in the *Stanford Social Innovation Review,* author Jim Bildner highlights "the actions of those who are rapidly pivoting their organizations to make a difference in the lives of others right now, in ways they had never envisioned just a month ago." With an eye on hundreds of nongovernmental organizations and nonprofits, Stanford can monitor the pace and care with which a variety of organizations have responded to the new demands of COVID-19.

"A number of our enterprises have shifted instantly, not to weather the storm, but to adapt their business models, distribution channels, and even their structure to respond to the ever-changing conditions on the ground," writes Bildner. He categorizes these shifts in three ways: "pop-ups," "pop-outs," and "push-throughs." These organizations are flexible, resilient in the face of obstacles, and creatively responding to new needs and constraints.

The pop-up Bildner highlights is impressive: Digital Bridge K–12 "spun out of two existing nonprofits." The first, EducationSuper-Highway (ESH), was focused on equipping under-resourced schools with broadband internet to help facilitate learning. When schools began rapidly closing in the Bay Area, they joined forces with 1 Million Project and within 30 days had mapped and started executing a plan to provide internet access "for tens of thousands of San Francisco Bay Area low-income students who are sheltering at home and have no access to broadband."

The article goes on to describe pop-outs (organizations that allow their physical spaces to be repurposed for the new and changing needs of their cities) and push-throughs (organizations that recognize the role they can play in giving structure to a newly emerging world). "Every organization must now think carefully about the world that will emerge and adapt now to the radically different models and behaviors that are likely to emerge. Organizations must simultaneously build resiliency and creativity." In other words, organizations must adopt a culture that values growth and learning, now more than ever.

Quoting Sam Gill, the chief program officer at the John S. and James L. Knight Foundation, Bildner emphasizes three things organizations must learn to do simultaneously: care for their workers and their families, handle relevant daily work, and most important, give "permission to look ahead" to those in an organization with an eye to innovation. Whatever your organization, these three areas of emphasis are at the heart of valuing growth.

If feasible, invite young people to be a part of the conversations about the fun work of looking ahead and innovating.

> **66** Three things organizations must learn to do simultaneously: care for their workers and their families, handle relevant daily work, and most important, give "permission to look ahead" to those in an organization with an eye to innovation. **99**

ACT ⟩ ON THE DATA: Take stock of whether your organization has succeeded in communicating your mission and extending your services in a virtual world—even consider asking others to "audit" you on this topic. Wherever you fall on the spectrum, consider researching webinars or emerging social mediums that may benefit your organization in the future. Be open-minded and adaptable about how technology might serve the people in your community.

ENCOURAGED BY THE CHALLENGE

James pursued music with an eager curiosity and intense commitment. He learned several instruments before he decided to focus his energy and time on flute in high school. One of his peers, Lily, was also a talented flutist.

As a young person who valued growth and learning, James wasn't discouraged by his more talented peer—he knew her talent would make him a better musician. Not only that, but the whole band would benefit. Week after week, James showed up to his early morning practices and his after-school band rehearsals.

Lily was younger than James and was shy. The two weren't overtly competitive *or* outrightly collaborative, but they shared an unspoken commitment to improving and honing their skills as individuals, though this work benefitted the whole ensemble. James "learned about musicality just by sitting next to her and paying attention to what she did" as she played.

On occasions, they were paired for duets. James said he "was driven to practice harder in order not to let her down or embarrass myself." His response is a good example of the dual value of being growthful: to learn and grow but also to avoid the negative consequences of falling behind in a rapidly shifting culture. When James was given the honor of first chair—a distinction indicating he was the most talented in his instru-ment—Lily wasn't resentful but seemed to take the challenge in stride, focusing on self-improvement without resentment, just as James had.

Describing obstacles that might discourage others—like talented peers, early morning lessons, long drives to extracurricular music commitments or hard no's from teachers, James said, "It never stopped me; it never made me think twice about my ability or my talent." Interested in self-improvement, creative in the face of perceived failures or setbacks, and with a disposition of constant learning and adapting, James embodies what it means to be growthful.

"I think it says a lot about my life on the whole, like, in the face of adversity, what have I done? Well, I think I've done a lot of cool things." James recognizes that being growthful is an important value to practice in a constantly and rapidly shifting world. He understands all this self-work as an investment in himself. Even if circumstances change unexpectedly, the lessons he's learned by virtue of pursuing music—hard work, perseverance, creative workarounds, self-knowledge, and difficult decision-making—will serve him well in any circumstances.

Individuals and organizations are wise to value growing and learning. It encourages not only a disposition of eager curiosity and constant learning but also a capacity for flexibility and adaptability. In a rapidly changing world, these capacities are not just about self-improvement but survival. Organizations that are unwilling to be uncomfortable—unwilling to be adaptable and creative learners—are not likely to last long amid rapidly changing circumstances. But even while they do exist, they are unlikely to attract or provide a meaningful experience for young people. Organizations most likely to attract or provide a meaningful experience for young people are those that recognize the capacity to grow and learn and seize opportunities to do so.

BRINGING IT ALL TOGETHER

Takeaways

1. Growth is a value that young people embrace and embody as a way of understanding that the world around them is constantly changing, and so remaining static is a liability. Keeping doors open and responding creatively to setbacks is about survival and flexibility. In fact, at its core, growth is about adaptability and flexibility. As a value that drives people, it is rooted in a sense that one is never quite done "becoming" who they are.

2. Any group that hopes to have young people as members can and should adopt practices that facilitate growth. Synagogues, schools, companies, and communities of all types have skill-building opportunities and perspectives to offer young people that can impact their whole lives, even outside the formal boundaries of those institutional walls or set gatherings.

3. Open-minded, flexible, and eager for opportunities for growth are three qualities that describe young people, and that can describe an organization that matches and mirrors the high value they place on growing.

4. According to Sam Gill, organizations must learn to do three things simultaneously: care for their workers and their families, handle relevant daily work, and most important, give "permission to look ahead" to those in an organization with an eye to innovation.

✓ Act on the Data

☐ Think about the "life skills" your organization can offer, even if it's not formally part of what you do. How can you offer this skill or perspective to young people in a way that both encourages self-improvement and helps prepare them for the ups and downs of the real world?

☐ Young people want to be a part of a culture that is growthful. The easiest way to implement and embody this value is by offering opportunities for learning and skill-building through your organization. What can or should a young person learn or gain by spending time with you or your group? How can you make this kind of learning more formal or official within your organization?

☐ Take stock of whether your organization has succeeded in communicating your mission and extending your services in a virtual world—even consider asking others to "audit" you on this topic. Wherever you fall on the spectrum, consider researching webinars or emerging social mediums that may benefit your organization in the future. Be open-minded and adaptable to how technology can serve the people in your community.

Reflect on Your Experience

- Rapid turnover affects many industries and fields: academia, media, publishing, fashion, tech, beauty, and more. Higher education and religious institutions have had to adapt to survive new and changing circumstances as well. If your organization hasn't felt this pressure yet, it's likely around the corner. What conversations can you have today that might set you up to start thinking flexibly, rather than fearfully, about what you can do to adapt and meet new needs in new ways?

- When have you felt stretched out of your comfort zone—either in an organizational leadership role or in your personal life—in a way that ultimately helped you learn and grow? How might that experience translate to the lives of those around you or to the organizations of which you are a part?

REFERENCES

Awake Youth Project. The information about AYP and the quotes from participants were taken from the "About Us" and "Offerings" tabs on the project's website.

Bildner, Jim. "Radically Adapting to the New World." *Stanford Social Innovation Review*, April 10, 2020.

McCabe, Sean. "Gen Z Optimistic about Future, EY Survey Finds." *Accounting Today*, September 6, 2017.

Poague, Emily. "Gen Z Is Shaping a New Era of Learning: Here's What You Should Know." *LinkedIn: The Learning Blog*, December 18, 2018.

CHAPTER 8

MEANINGFUL

At age 13, Alec Gewirtz said he "came under the spell of certain voices, like [Ralph Waldo] Emerson, who were deeply curious about the largest questions of life, and how revelatory experiences could speak to these highest questions. I was unsure exactly where they fit into the religious landscape, but I was totally captivated by them."

Alec said as he moved into high school and later college, he was seeing "profound emotional wounds in the people around me. I had the unavoidable sense that people were not living the deeply rewarding lives that they could be living."

Alec himself came from what he described as a "nonreligious family. My parents were Jewish, but I had no bar mitzvah, because it conflicted with basketball practice. We had a Christmas tree."

Similar to many young people we have surveyed, although Alec was not attached to such traditional institutional religious entities as a synagogue, church, or mosque, he found himself asking the sorts of questions those institutions have been wrestling with for millennia.

Alec enrolled at Princeton University as a religious studies major. "Religious organizations have historically met profound human needs, and nonreligious people in the present don't have many parallel institutions to meet these same needs," he explained. "To create such institutions, we need to study some of the past institutions that were so successful in doing so. Even if I can't borrow comprehensively from them, I can take inspiration and concrete lessons from them."

Alec noted many others at Princeton on a quest similar to his own: to find a convening space where they could engage in the meaningful conversations they were craving. "There is and always has been a large number of people who have not been in tune as regularly as they would like with the most profound aspects of human experience and want to have structures to make those experiences as rich and deeply meaningful as they could be," he said.

Alec sensed a need for a nonreligious structure where he and his fellow students could wrestle with human experience at a deeper level. Not finding one, he set out to create one.

MEANING MAKING
Insights from Springtide Research

In this book, which is dedicated to exploring and unpacking the values that young people practice and—importantly—want the organizations they join to practice too, many instances of meaning making have surfaced.

- Any gesture that grasps for "more" is a practice of meaning making.

- Any impulse toward something beyond what's simply expected, easy, or at the surface is a practice of meaning making.

- Any pursuit of the transcendent—whether in creative expression or commitments to causes, prayer, or personal relationships—is a practice of meaning making.

Each of the values highlighted in this book are specific instances of these gestures, impulses, and pursuits, and they all point to one overwhelming conclusion: Young people want meaningful lives.

Being accountable, inclusive, authentic, welcoming, impactful, relational, and growthful are all ways of adding meaning to a person's life and to the lives of others. They are virtues and values that call a person to something more real, more open, more thoughtful, and more considerate of the world around them. They are attempts to live a more purposeful, more *meaningful* life.

This capacity to grasp for what is beyond—to pursue virtue and practice values that contribute to the well-being of self and other—is a uniquely human capacity. Other chapters have demonstrated the way meaningfulness is embodied through accountable community and supportive inclusion. They have shown the way meaning making is lived out in creative self-expression and in opportunities for safe participation. This book has pointed out the way meaningfulness looks like environmental activism, social relationships, and the desire for constant growth.

But the value of meaningfulness is expressed in another way only hinted at in previous chapters. It is the explicit way that people pursue questions (and sometimes answers) about the nature of truth, beauty, goodness, justice, suffering, and so on. It is that philosophical impulse to ask *why* coupled with the human impulse to live out the answer. It is the way one person can transcend their particular experience by finding themselves bound up with the stories, ideas, and activities of others. This was the kind of meaning-making work Alec was determined to take up as he pursued life's big questions.

But this desire for significant meaning is not unique to Alec's story. When Springtide surveyed young people about the value of meaningfulness in their lives, we found that 65% of respondents say it is important for organizations they participate in to provide opportunities for them to clarify, articulate, and act on their personal mission in life.

of young people surveyed say it is important for organizations they participate in to **provide opportunities for them to clarify, articulate, and act on their personal mission in life.**

When asked about current or future work, nearly 50% say that work is not worth doing if it has no meaning. More than 40% say they avoid activities that don't mean anything to them, and that joining an organization is a waste of time if they don't find meaning in its activities. To put it directly, the data are clear that if you are not helping young people find meaning in the ways they engage with your organization, you shouldn't expect them to stick around for long . . . or to even show up in the first place.

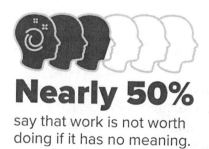

Nearly 50%
say that work is not worth doing if it has no meaning.

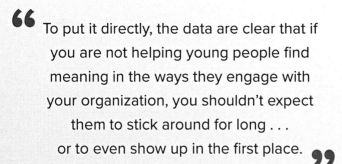

> **"** To put it directly, the data are clear that if you are not helping young people find meaning in the ways they engage with your organization, you shouldn't expect them to stick around for long . . . or to even show up in the first place. **"**

Additionally, over half (54%) of young people agree that it is important to live according to their faith values. This is a significant statistic that tells us that whatever young people believe in, they want to live out and practice it in their lives. In other words, they aren't interested in rituals, routines, or work that isn't rooted in or connected to some greater purpose. Significantly, 25% of young people Springtide surveyed feel as though their life rarely or never has meaning or purpose. That doesn't mean they aren't seeking it—it means they have needs that organizations, peers, and trusted adults can help them satisfy.

The examples that follow highlight and unpack the trend toward meaningfulness as a value for young people, including how certain individuals, organizations, and educational institutions are responding innovatively to meet this desire.

Making Meaning with Music

Together with collaborator Rev. Sue Phillips, Angie Thurston and Casper ter Kuile produced the *How We Gather* report while students at Harvard Divinity School. This report highlights an emerging trend among millennials and young adults: a trend *toward* community and meaning making, which was an especially surprising finding against the backdrop of steady religious disaffiliation for the past decade.

They discovered and studied nontraditional spaces answering this call: workout gyms providing personal accountability, arts movements promoting social and personal transformation, grown-up summer camps as creative communities imbued with ritual and retreat. This report notes six recurring themes in the organizations they studied: community, personal transformation, social transformation, purpose finding, creativity, and accountability.

In the introduction to their report, the authors describe the way young people are forging something new. Despite checking the "none" box on quantitative surveys when it comes to religious practices, young people are seeking meaning. In fact . . .

> **when they say they are not looking for a faith community, [they] might mean they are not interested in belonging to an institution with religious creed as the threshold. However, they are decidedly looking for spirituality and community in combination, and feel they can't lead a meaningful life without it.**

Ter Kuile, writing in *Pacific Standard* in 2019, breaks these categories and spaces down even further. He notes a statistic reported in June 2018 by *Vice:* "Eighty percent of these young people have a sense of spirituality, believing in some cosmic power, while seven in 10 are looking for spirituality but think organized religion is not relevant." And then he asks the all-important question: How are young people finding meaning? How are they "caring for their souls?"

At this point, ter Kuile observes a fluid pattern that can and does pervade many different types of organizations and social gatherings: the way *music* can connect people and give meaning. "The most common 'spiritual technology' for connection is music," he writes, noting that traditional institutions for meaning making and meaning giving, like organized religion, haven't met young people's expectations.

Drawing on a story from his own experience, he recalls a time when undergraduates in a dormitory he oversaw created a space after a student died by suicide. "His friends wanted to process their emotions together. . . . They suggested bringing a guitar, and hosted a gathering of grieving—telling stories and singing together."

Something about music transcends traditional boundaries: music has form and structure but also emotion and flexibility—meaning can be interpreted differently by each person, and even by the same person at different points in their life. Though music may not be the cause for gathering at your own organization, the principle this illustrates can apply broadly.

Young people are seeking meaningful experiences wherever they go. If one is not provided—as in the case of students grieving in the space of their dorms—they will create it. **Music is one of the tools anyone can use to make space for meaning, but there are others: technology, poetry, ritual, and more. Many of the examples and tips provided in this book are ways to bring meaning-making practices to spaces not always associated with that task.** Perhaps music can be incorporated into some practices at your organization. Alternatively, maybe you can use onboarding as a way of creating a sense of belonging and welcoming. Perhaps you can use social media as a medium for cultivating authentic relationships. Maybe your group can hold space for raising environmental consciousness: these are *all* ways of bringing meaning-making practices into your organization.

ACT > **ON THE DATA:** Sixty-five percent of young people say it is important for organizations they participate in to provide opportunities for them to clarify, articulate, and act on their personal mission in life. Music has a particular kind of power for creating meaning and connecting communities. Can you imagine ways your organization might harness the power of music to help young people clarify their sense of purpose?

ASKING THE BIG QUESTIONS, LIVING THE BIG ANSWERS

In *Belonging: Reconnecting America's Loneliest Generation*, Springtide reports a pattern noted by other researchers: young people are more isolated, disconnected, stressed, and lonely than ever before. Research for this book found that 25% of the young people surveyed feel as though their life rarely or never has meaning or purpose.

Whether or not they feel their life has meaning at the moment, young people are *seeking* meaning. As in the example of music, they are seeking all kinds of meaning *outside* conventional spaces like religion, family, or even work. **New organizations and groups are emerging to fill this void and to facilitate meaning-making practices in the lives of young people. Part of being an organization that helps young people cultivate meaning in their lives is understanding where a sense of meaning and purpose comes from.**

Dr. Laurie Santos, a professor of psychology at Yale University, teaches the most popular course in Yale's 319-year history. "While most large lectures at Yale don't exceed 600 students, Psychology and the Good Life had enrolled 1,182," a *Business Insider* article reports. This course, Psychology and the Good Life, focuses broadly on the practices and pitfalls of pursuing happiness.

Using brain and cognitive behavioral science, Santos invites students to recognize why the brain might *believe* that money, fame, a promotion, or a new gadget will make a person happy but why—in fact—the "next" thing always disappoints. In addition to learning why winning the lottery or an Olympic medal won't make a person ultimately happy, students also learn practices that actually can, scientifically and statistically, increase their happiness—in other words, habits that can help facilitate a sense of meaning and purpose, no matter the circumstances.

> " Why this universal fascination with the question of happiness? Because it captures one of the deepest and most common longings of the human heart. It is one of those questions that grounds and transcends individual human experience, and connects people to one another. "

This course has been popular not only with students but people of all ages around the world. Santos has launched a podcast, *The Happiness Lab,* that unpacks these themes in conversation with other experts and practitioners. Yale offers a modified version of the original course on Coursera called The Science of Well-Being that anyone can take.

Why this universal fascination with the question of happiness? Because it captures one of the deepest and most common longings of the human heart. It is one of those questions that grounds and transcends individual human experience and connects people to one another. It's the same as the question of meaning and purpose—the assumption being that if you find one, you have the other. They are interchangeable. If the winning lottery ticket won't bring you meaning, purpose, and happiness, then what will?

A *New York Times* interview with Santos gets at some of the recurring themes that come up as antidotes to a sense of meaninglessness: "Students want to change, to be happier themselves, and to change the culture here on campus," Dr. Santos said in an interview. "With one in four students at Yale taking it, if we see good habits, things like students showing more gratitude, procrastinating less, increasing social connections, we're actually seeding change in the school's culture."

In other words, practicing many of the values highlighted in this book—accountability, social impact, authenticity, relationality—are all ways of finding meaning. The *Times* article continues, quoting Alannah Maynez, age 19: "In reality, a lot of us are anxious, stressed, unhappy, numb. . . . The fact that a class like this has such large interest speaks to how tired students are of numbing their emotions—both positive and negative—so they can focus on their work."

It is clear just how urgently and desperately people, *especially* young people, are seeking these paths toward purpose. In 300 years of class offerings at a world-renowned institution, students are signing up in droves to read and discuss living a more meaningful life. But the practices that emerge out of this reading and discussing are not confined to the classroom. Gratitude, accountability, relationships, creativity—these are values any organization can and should take up to add meaning to their group.

ACT ⟩ ON THE DATA: A quarter of young people report feeling that their life rarely or never has meaning. But young people—in fact, all people—seek meaning. Consider listening to *The Happiness Lab* podcast or signing up for The Science of Well-Being, a free course on Coursera, to learn more about how to add small, intentional practices to your organization to add meaning to your group and to the lives of young people around you.

CREATING MEANINGFUL SPACES

Alec Gewirtz, like his Princeton peers, wanted communal spaces where they might articulate and clarify ideas for acting on a personal mission in life. In his sophomore year, Alec started a listserv essay in the form of a Sunday letter sent out asking a question that "people around me seemed to be grappling with," regarding such topics as past friendships, or how to keep from growing apart from parents. The letter attracted 400 subscribers, with a 75% open rate. Alec sensed a need for "something bigger."

He began Workshop No. 1 in response. Alec told *The Daily Princetonian* in 2018: "I started Workshop No. 1 because there wasn't a venue on campus where people could reflect on how to build more fulfilling lives. People needed a space where they could step outside their weekly routines to recapture a sense of purpose, and for most students there wasn't that venue."

"People want guidance," Alec told Springtide. "They want a framework in which they can address questions that inevitably arise in life, stories to situate those questions, principles to address. There aren't attempts to do that on my radar. I say that as someone now very much slowly trying to ready myself to do something . . . more."

"I know that wherever it takes me, it won't take me in isolation. The need is so enormous; I can't pretend to meet it even for one population by myself. Essentially, I see it as an artistic, intellectual, organizational, and community-building project to create institutions people so desperately want."

Alec isn't naïve about the challenges in creating such spaces. "I'm not equipped to do all of that. There is tremendous cultural fear of any new institutions in this space being somehow cult-like. There is lots to guard against in trying to create these institutions.

"I am a religion major because I think that I want to devote my life to creating values-based communities for religiously unaffiliated people of our generation," Alec said.

"I don't know where it's going—it's totally plausible that the sorts of ideas that I try to promote, the stories to bring those ideas to life can live alongside religious commitment. I'm not allergic to that possibility," said Alec, who at the time of our interview was living in a L'Arche[1] community in Toronto that included five people with severe intellectual difficulties.

"I met with an evangelical pastor in the Midwest. His advice to me was not to be afraid about throwing up walls around what I'm doing. People do want to organize around identities. To create something sustainable, there needs to be some sort of identity, perhaps around lacking religious identification at least in part. That's where I am for now. But what we promote may fit alongside people in more liberal religious communities. Maybe intergenerational efforts are needed."

"I am approaching my reading, writing, living, with the goal of helping to meet, in whatever small way I can, these profound human needs."

Our research confirms that Alec is on to something that aligns with the values of many young people such as himself. It's clear that young people are drawn to be a part of groups and organizations that connect them to something larger than themselves. And if they have to create those organizations themselves, they will.

Young people want to see their story as bound up with the story of others, to see their work as meaningful, and they want their daily work to help them to clarify and act on their personal mission in the world. To put it in sociological terms, while the formal mission or tasks of an organization can be mundane—that is to say, "regular" or "not spiritual" in nature—it must in some way connect them to "something more." It must help move them beyond themselves as individuals and engage the big questions that both transcend and ground individual experience.

---

[1] L'Arche is an international organization that brings people with and without intellectual disabilities together to live in community with one another.

Bringing It All Together

Takeaways

1. Any gesture that grasps for "more" is a practice of meaning making. Any impulse toward something beyond what's simply expected, easy, or at the surface is a practice of meaning making. Any pursuit of the transcendent—whether in creative expression or commitments to environmentalism, prayer, or personal relationships—is a practice of meaning making. Each of the values highlighted in this book are specific instances of these gestures, impulses, and pursuits.

2. Music is one of the tools anyone can use to make space for meaning, but there are others: technology, poetry, ritual, and more. Indeed, many of the examples and tips provided in this book are ways to bring meaning-making practices to spaces not always associated with that task.

3. New organizations and groups are emerging to fill a void and facilitate meaning-making practices in the lives of young people. And part of being an organization that helps young people cultivate meaning in their lives is understanding where a sense of meaning and purpose comes from.

4. Why this universal fascination with the question of happiness? Because it captures one of the deepest and most common longings of the human heart. It is one of those questions that grounds and transcends individual human experience and connects people to one another.

√ Act on the Data

☐ Sixty-five percent of young people say it is important for organizations they participate in to provide opportunities for them to clarify, articulate, and act on their personal mission in life. Music has a particular kind of power for creating meaning and connecting communities. Can you imagine any ways your organization might harness the power of music to help young people clarify their sense of purpose?

☐ A quarter of young people report feeling that their life rarely or never has meaning. But young people—in fact, all people—seek meaning. Consider listening to *The Happiness Lab* podcast or signing up for The Science of Well-Being, a free course on Coursera, to learn more about how to add small, intentional practices to your organization to add meaning to your group and to the lives of young people around you.

Reflect on Your Experience

- If you've read all the chapters in this book, which stands out to you as the most immediately applicable for integrating into your organization's culture? If you haven't finished reading, which intrigues or intimidates you? Why do you think this is?

- How would you define the meaningful aspects of your life? What would you point to as practices, people, or organizations that bring meaning and purpose to your days? Once you have a sense of these things for yourself, invite others to reflect on this question and share your reflections as well.

- Have you, like Alec, ever felt like you had a need or desire but the outlet for it didn't yet exist? What did you do to meet the need you perceived in yourself or others at that time?

REFERENCES

Leighton, Mara. "Yale's Most Popular Class Ever Is Available Free Online—and the Topic Is How to Be Happier in Your Daily Life." *Business Insider*, April 10, 2020.

Marans, Yael. "Secular Group Workshop No. 1 Brings Reflection, Community to U. Community." *Daily Princetonian*, October 22, 2018.

Shimer, David. "Yale's Most Popular Class Ever: Happiness." *The New York Times*, January 26, 2018.

ter Kuile, Casper. "How Gen Z Is Solving America's Crisis of Isolation." *Standard Pacific*, May 6, 2019.

"The Science of Well-Being." This online course taught by Dr. Laurie Santos and offered by Yale University is available free from the Coursera website.

Thurston, Angie, and Casper ter Kuile. *How We Gather.* This report, along with others in the series—*Care of Souls, Something More, Faithful,* and *December Gathering*—can be found on the website of the Sacred Design Lab.

CONCLUSION

Throughout the chapters of *Meaning Making,* we have introduced values that young people tell us are important to them. In other words, values they tell us are *meaningful,* whether in personal practice, embodied by the organizations they join, or—more often than not—both.

This desire for a meaningful life is as old as time. A unique feature of our shared humanity, we have religious and political systems, clubs and sports, causes and commitments that all help shape and channel this desire toward an end that can satisfy. In this sense, meaningfulness is subjective: for each individual, the exact path to a meaningful life will look different.

And for many young people today, the traditional systems for exploring meaning don't hold appeal. Trust in nearly every traditional sector—education, business, religion, government, and so on—is down, and not just among young people. But the desire for meaning, even meaning *outside* these traditional institutions and structures, hasn't diminished.

It has just found new spaces, new outlets, and new expressions. Many of these expressions are captured in this book.

Accountability is about clear expectations, shared purpose, and forums for feedback.

To be **inclusive** is to be welcoming, supportive, and respectful.

Authenticity is characterized by the ability to be totally oneself, without worry about performing a certain way.

The value of **welcoming** is both a gesture of hospitality and a felt experience of belonging.

Being **impactful** is about actively engaging key social issues and thoughtfully minimizing harm.

Practicing being **relational** includes thoughtful investments in both bridging and bonding connections.

Valuing **growth** means encouraging a disposition of curiosity and learning, as well a capacity for flexibility and adaptability.

And finally, the value of **meaning** making—the theme of this book—is about grasping for more, moving beyond what's expected, pursuing the big questions and living them out. All the values highlighted in this book are specific instances of these gestures, impulses, and pursuits.

We know that young people want rich and meaningful lives.

People used to find meaning in many places. They would find a sense of community in places like churches, synagogues, and mosques. They would find identity and authenticity within family life, and seek community in their work or hobbies.

For many, these traditional spaces continue to be deeply life-giving and formative. But many others are seeking accountability, inclusivity, authenticity—in fact, all the values described in this book—in new and unexpected spaces. Perhaps they are looking for these things from *your* organization, and perhaps you have felt this desire from the young people in your life and work, and have sometimes felt ill-equipped for the task of embodying these values or creating spaces for young people to practice them.

Through both definitions and data, with individual stories and spotlight examples, we hope this book has helped clarify some of the values that drive young people today. In clarifying these values, we ultimately hope we have helped clarify the ways you can serve the young people in your midst.

Springtide™
RESEARCH INSTITUTE

WE'RE LISTENING TO YOUNG PEOPLE. AND TO YOU.

We exist at the intersection of religious and human experience in the lives of young people. And we're here to listen.

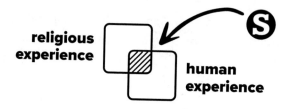

religious experience

human experience

We combine quantitative and qualitative research to reflect and amplify the lived realities of young people as they navigate shifting social, cultural, and religious landscapes. Delivering fresh data and actionable insights, we equip those who care about young people to care better.

Join the conversation.
springtideresearch.org

Connect with us on social media. Follow @WeAreSpringtide on Facebook, Instagram, and Twitter.